They Dreamed of
Horses

They Dreamed of
Horses

Careers for Horse Lovers

KAY FRYDENBORG

Photographs by Tanya Wood

Walker and Company
New York

For Woody, who taught me so much

First published in the United States of America in 1994 by Walker
Publishing Company, Inc.

Published simultaneously in Canada by Thomas Allen & Son Canada,
Limited, Markham, Ontario

Library of Congress Cataloging-in-Publication Data
Frydenborg, Kay.
They dreamed of horses : careers for horse lovers / Kay Frydenborg ;
photographs by Tanya Wood.
p.   cm.
Includes bibliographical references (p.   ) and index.
ISBN 0-8027-8283-3 (cloth edition). —ISBN 0-8027-8284-1
(reinforced library edition)
1. Horse industry—Vocational guidance—Juvenile literature.
2. Horsemen and horsewomen—Juvenile literature.   3. Women animal
specialists—Juvenile literature.   [1. Horse industry—Vocational
guidance.   2. Horsemen and horsewomen.   3. Women animal specialists.
4. Occupations.   5. Vocational guidance.]   I. Wood, Tanya, ill.
II. Title.
SF285.25.F78   1994
636.1′0023—dc20   93-33023
                                                          CIP
                                                          AC

*Diagrams on pages 16 and 59
by Erik Nils Frydenborg.*

Book design by Claire Naylon Vaccaro

Printed in the United States of America

2   4   6   8   10   9   7   5   3   1

Contents

Acknowledgments

THIS BOOK COULD not have been written without the help of the horsewomen whose stories are told here. I wish to thank all of them for their time and generous support, and for being so passionate about their work that they were willing to talk to me about their lives at length.

My thanks, also, go to Tanya Wood, whose excellent photography has accompanied so much of my work and has never failed to enhance a project.

For all their helpful comments, ideas, and understanding, I thank my horse-loving friends Marge, Judy, Maria, and Karen, and my trainers (and dear friends) Terri and Chris, along with Mike, my farrier.

My appreciation goes to Walker and Company for giving me the opportunity to do this book, and to Mary Perrotta Rich for her enthusiasm and her perceptive guidance.

Above all, I thank my family for their support throughout this project: Laurel, for being both a willing model and a picky editor, and for sharing my love of words and of horses; Erik, my artist, for his talent and his willingness to step in when I needed him at nearly the last minute; and Lans, for helping me in so many ways, and for being there when I needed a shoulder to cry on or a voice of reason.

1

Who Dreams of Horses?

THERE IS A certain kind of person who seems to be born loving horses. She can hardly remember a time when being with horses didn't seem like the ultimate dream. She reads books about horses, collects miniature horse figures, and creates endless games and fantasies starring the tiny equines. Perhaps she follows the careers of her favorite horses the way some kids study baseball cards. Maybe she comes from a "horsey" background and has the opportunity to ride and care for horses, but just as likely she is the only one in her family who knows a bay from a chestnut, and she lives in a town or city miles from the nearest pasture. Still, unlikely as it may seem to everyone else, she knows that someday she will find a way to be with horses.

Maybe this is your dream, too. Maybe you think it's an impossible dream, but there are ways to have a life with horses without being a millionaire or even a talented rider or trainer. Whatever your particular talents or interests, there is probably a way to combine them with some type of work with horses. The advice "Do what you love, the money will follow" is true for everyone. If there is one thing the women in this book have in common, it is a passion for horses. And like most passions, it is not easy to explain its source, but usually the attraction begins early in childhood.

What is it about horses that makes us love them so? Horsepeople are animal lovers, of course, and they usually enjoy the company of dogs, cats, and other furry creatures, but there's something special about horses. The horse is the only domestic animal that combines the strength and power of an ox, the grace and elegance of a cat, and the kindness and generosity of a dog. It possesses a noble spirit and an uncanny intelligence that, for those who share the passion, sets the horse apart from all other animals. A horse responds best not to brute force, but to patience, understanding, and the ability on the part of those who work with him to "think like a horse." For horsepeople, physical strength is of little importance. A small woman may be better able to relate to a 1,200-pound Thoroughbred than can a tall, muscular man. Astride a swift and powerful horse, a puny human becomes as fast as the wind and as strong as the earth itself.

The horse shares a history with humans that goes at least as far back as three thousand years before the time of Christ. In fact, horseback riding may predate the invention of the wheel, thus being the first significant innovation in human transportation.

Until the coming of the internal combustion engine in the late nineteenth century, all of society was dependent on equine abilities for farming, transportation, sport, pleasure, and warfare. As machines rapidly began to replace horse labor in the early twentieth century, the demand for horses for show and sport increased.

Today is a better time for most horses than any since the history of humans and horses became forever intertwined. Horses are not just an outdated labor-saving device or a frivolous pastime; they are big business. In recent years American horse owners have spent about fifteen billion dollars annually on their five and a half million horses. Horse sports attract more than 110 million spectators in America each year, and more than 27 million Americans over age twelve ride horses, more than half on a regular basis. Considering the horse's importance in our society and economy, it's really not surprising that so many people are able to find careers working with horses. It's plain to see that the human love affair with horses is here to stay.

Many women and girls seem to have a natural affinity for these powerful, keenly sensitive, and gentle creatures—of the people actively involved with horses on a day-to-day basis, 80 percent are women. The vast majority of U.S. horses are found in backyard paddocks, tended not by professionals but by women who love them, women for whom owning a horse is the answer to a lifelong dream. And in larger boarding stables where the horses of suburbanites and city dwellers are kept, you will often find an easy camaraderie among females from six to sixty, and from all walks of life. This passion knows no boundaries. Horses bring these women together in a way that schools, jobs, and other pursuits never could.

Some of these women, through sheer determination and ingenuity, have found a way to merge passion and occupation. By combining their own special talents with a deep love of horses, many women today are inventing new careers for themselves. Hard work and a commitment to their goals are what all of these horsewomen share, and the rewards are as various as the horses they love.

2

Trish Nixon

Equine Artist

TRISH NIXON OF Lexington, Kentucky, has loved both horses and art since earliest childhood. "My mother has said that before I could even talk, I was fascinated by horses." When she was very young, Trish's family lived in an isolated rural area of Pennsylvania. "Our paperboy could only get to our house on horseback. From what my mother says, I would wait by the door for the paperboy to come every day just so I could get a look at his horse." Since she was old enough to hold a pencil, Trish has also loved drawing. Early loves run deep, and it was only natural for Trish to combine her two passions as she was growing up. "I was always one of those kids who got in trouble for constantly sitting in my classes sketching horses," she recalls, "and I distinctly remember an art teacher telling me I wouldn't be able to make a living painting horses. Another teacher said if I drew one more horse she would scream, she was so sick of seeing my horses. So from an early age, I was discouraged from horse art."

Many girls spend endless hours drawing horses as a way to express their deep longing to have a horse of their own, but Trish kept right on drawing after her parents gave her her first horse at age sixteen. "My parents figured that with cars and boys, I'd lose interest in horses soon enough," she says with a laugh. "But that just made the 'horse fever' stronger, and I started taking riding lessons." Eventually Trish began giving riding lessons to beginners, and also started showing her horses at local hunter-jumper competitions. One day it dawned on her that the horse shows would provide a perfect gallery for her artwork. At the next show she attended, she got permission from the show manager to set up her easel next to her trailer. She sketched some of the show horses during the long wait between classes, and her work soon began to attract the attention of other competitors.

After graduation from high school, Trish went to art school. An associate degree in commercial art landed her a job in advertising. That experience, far from being a way of selling out to commercial pressures, provided invaluable experience she was able to use in marketing her "real" work. When Trish left the ad agency job in 1988 to devote herself full-time to her art, she knew how to publicize her business. "I knew how to market myself," she says. "I knew what magazines to buy space in, I knew how to write advertising copy, and I knew how to present my information. I've gotten responses to my ads from all over—Hawaii, New Mexico, Wisconsin, even Alaska. Advertising definitely pays." Most of her business still comes from horse shows, though, and word-of-mouth promotion from satisfied clients. "When I first started this," she says, "it amazed me how people would go out of their way to help me get more business."

In the beginning, most of Trish's clients were owners and riders on the hunter-jumper circuit. This elegant and exciting sport, in which sleek horses and traditionally dressed riders jump courses of fences as perfectly as they possibly can, attracts amateurs and professionals all over the country. Many travel to horse shows nearly every weekend during the showing season. Some of the most serious competitors even travel halfway across the country to pursue their sport year-round, showing in the Northeast in summer, the Southeast or West in summer. In many ways it is a small world. People who spend a lot of their leisure time at horse shows get to know one another, and if someone "discovers" a favorite artist like Trish Nixon, word can travel fast.

A typical horseperson might want to have one special horse captured in a commissioned portrait, or a young rider's parents might present her with a Christmas portrait of her favorite pony. "When a person has a young horse who starts doing well at shows, the owner is as proud of that animal as he would be of a child who had gone to college and become a doctor," says Trish. "He's already invested thousands in the horse, its tack, and boarding, so the fee I charge, about

five hundred to six hundred dollars for a standard portrait, is just a drop in the bucket."

At this point in her career Trish's subjects include—in addition to famous hunters and jumpers and backyard ponies—racehorses, draft horses, warmbloods, chunky Morgan carriage horses, Andalusians with their animated movements and long, flowing manes and tails, and nearly every other breed and discipline in the horse world. In 1989 the prestigious Pennsylvania National Horse Show commissioned Trish to create the show's official poster. She also completes many commissioned portraits of dogs, from feisty little Jack Russell terriers to the sleek Dobermans and dalmations commonly kept as stable pets. Trish also produces a line of notecards available in tack shops across the country, and many people who purchase a portrait of their horse or dog will also buy notecards the artist makes by reducing the original drawing.

Greeting cards are her newest venture. Increasing business from owners of Andalusian horses led to a feature article in early 1992 in *Conquistadors* magazine. That, in turn, caught the attention of the greeting card and stationery companies. The product line will include notecards, miniposters, and gift wrap based on Trish Nixon designs. "The successes I've had," she says, "have given me courage to explore new directions for my work." In the beginning, Trish traveled considerable distances to horse shows to make contacts and generate commissions. But since establishing her base of operations in Lexington, a horse lover's paradise, she finds little need to travel. The famous Kentucky Horse Park hosts equine activities year-round, and such premier events as the Rolex/Kentucky Horse Trials are right in her backyard. Keeneland, a major racetrack, is another source of subject matter.

"I go to Keeneland in the early morning and watch the horses work out, and hang around the barn and paddocks," she says. "I have gotten some great photos and met several well-known jockeys, too." Trish works in graphite or a combination of watercolor and pastel. The black-and-white graphite drawings are very popular because the medium highlights the bone structure and expression of the animal. She works from photographs, which she takes herself wherever possible, in order to produce an accurate likeness. It's important, she says, that she displays her work at horse shows rather than art shows. "That way, I can 'meet' my subject, take reference photos, and watch the horse compete. This adds a lot to the kind of feeling I can put into his expression—knowing if the animal is quiet, high-strung, devilish, or whatever." Her work is very detailed, right down to the smallest item of tack or anatomy. Horsepeople will notice if a bit is incorrectly connected to a bridle or the reins are too wide, and they demand accuracy. "I concentrate on the horse's bone structure and the expression in his face," she says. "Horses have incredibly expressive eyes, and I do everything I can to capture that. I perfected drawing them by just doing hundreds of horse eyes." It takes the artist up to fifteen hours to produce a typical portrait.

Aspiring equine artists should first learn the basic techniques at a good art school, advises Trish. Even though your instructors will not be likely to encourage you to draw horses, the techniques of illustration and design you will learn in art school are necessary for any kind of portrait work. But don't expect to set the world on fire financially right away.

"Horse people are a cliquey bunch," says Trish, "and they'll have to see your stuff over and over before they really believe in you. That means you might have to practically give your portraits away in the beginning. But if you find the right niche and develop a good following, and if you make your stuff unique in some way, eventually it is possible to make a decent living." Trish's prices have gone up every year since she started her business, and she expects that they will continue to go up. Many people have suggested to her that she double her portrait fees, but she says, "I really would hate to do that. *I wouldn't be able to afford that, if I were the one commissioning the portrait. I want to keep my stuff affordable for the average owner.*" She considers her prices to be in the middle range for equine artists, with some of the top names in the field earning as much as fifty or sixty thousand dollars a year. And she considers her business to be part-time, because, "even though I put in a lot of hours, if I want to go riding I go, and I just don't draw that day." Trish's business netted a profit of eleven thousand dollars last year. She emphasizes the importance of investing in advertising and exhibiting one's work at shows, and cautions that an aspiring artist should plan to have at least

five to eight thousand dollars to comfortably get her through the "tough times" in the early days of her business. The main reason to become an equine artist, she insists, is because you love drawing horses, not because you want to get rich.

"It's something I've wanted to do since I can remember knowing how to hold a pencil, and I couldn't just keep hanging my drawings in my own house forever. It's satisfying when I mail a customer a piece, and within five minutes of opening it they call to say it's beautiful, and they can't believe how much it looks like their horse. My greatest compliment is when someone sees a portrait and recognizes the horse in it." Working in her home studio more than ten hours a day, bending over her drawing table, surrounded by photographs, pencils, brushes, and preliminary studies of her equine subjects, Trish finds she often has little or no time to ride anymore. She brought her elderly, beloved Morgan with her from Pennsylvania to her new home in Lexington. Since then she has acquired a younger horse, a handsome bay Thoroughbred, and she does as much with him as time permits, attending local dressage clinics, taking lessons, and just riding for fun. She still dreams of one day owning an Andalusian horse, the breed she has most loved since childhood, but for now her life is more than full. "Even when I don't have time to ride," she says, "I want to be able to look out of my studio window and see horses. I want to see something beautiful."

3

Tina Craumer

Horse-drawn Carriage Service

THE HARNESS AND carriage are gleaming ebony and silver, the velvet seats are plush crimson, and the huge gray gelding is polished, every hair in place. The bride and groom, seated aloft on the soft seat, are flushed with excitement, as if transported to another time by the very elegance and romance of the moment. As the wedding party gathers, the young woman in the black woolen uniform complete with top hat glances at the high clouds in the sky and reviews her route from the church through the center of the town to the country club where the reception will be held. She hopes the rain will hold off; she and her husband got up before dawn to begin readying the equipment and bathing the muddy Percheron, and now you'd never know that yesterday Joey found the muddiest spot in the pasture in which to roll. Now he's shifting his weight impatiently from one massive hoof to the other, and his driver knows he's ready to get to his job.

Tina Craumer has owned horses most of her life, but only the

first, a Chincoteague pony her parents bought when she was seven, was given to her. Her parents didn't own land on which to keep the pony, but her uncle did, and Tina remembers carting the tiny pony there in the back of a pickup truck. From then on, she rode nearly every weekend. There was no money for riding lessons, so she had to teach herself to ride and care for the pony, with a little help from her father and uncle. "I'd just go off through the woods with my pony," says Tina, but by the time she was about fourteen or fifteen she had outgrown the pony. "My parents said I could only have another if I raised the money to buy it myself." So the summer before she turned sixteen, the determined teenager set out to do just that. She worked all summer picking tomatoes on a local farm, and also made tissue paper flowers, which she sold. She managed to save $75, and then found a quarter horse/Morgan yearling that she could purchase for that amount. Misty also went to live on Tina's uncle's farm, and when the filly was old enough Tina broke her to saddle with the help of books her uncle gave her. Five years later, at age twenty-one, Tina took out an $800 loan to buy her first quarter horse mare, which she then bred. She still has that first foal, now fourteen years old, but she sold five or six others that the mare produced. Eventually Tina traded the mare back for a quarter horse stallion, now twenty-one, and her fledgling horse-breeding business was off and running.

"I always loved anything and everything to do with horses," says Tina. Like many other girls in love with horses, she dreamed of a career as a trainer or jockey, or maybe a veterinarian. "I wanted to study equine science in college, but my parents really discouraged me from doing that. At that time, it just wasn't considered a proper career for a girl, at least not where I came from." Even so, the horses continued to be the central focus of her life, shared later by her husband and two children.

Clark Craumer was no stranger to horses when he and Tina married, since his parents had owned a riding stable when he was growing up. "He lived on a farm and knew a lot about animals," says Tina. In addition to being a full partner in the carriage business, Clark raises goats and helps tend to the multiple chores of a working farm. Both of the children (a daughter, fifteen, and a son, ten) currently ride and show quarter horses in 4-H and open shows. When the Craumers moved from a small farm to the larger one they now own, they began boarding horses for other owners. One of the boarders was a woman who ran a horse-drawn carriage service in the small city of York, Pennsylvania, who began keeping her two Percheron carriage horses with Tina. A year later, when the woman made plans to move out of the area, she asked Tina and her husband if they were interested in buying the carriage business. They jumped at the chance, and in two or three months both learned the basics of driving the huge, gentle draft horses.

"We started out here on the farm where it's quiet," says Tina, "but pretty soon we went right out into traffic, starting with the less busy roads and working our way up to dealing with city traffic, news media, cameras, lights, and other things that can be scary for the horses." The Craumers started with a reproduction of an antique carriage purchased from a supplier in Indiana, but they have recently acquired a 120-year-old carriage, which they are in the process of refurbishing. They also operate a horse-drawn sleigh in the winter, which can accommodate up to fifteen passengers for an old-fashioned ride across snowy fields. "We've brought Santa in the sled to special holiday events," explains Tina, "and we've also taken kids with Santa to a Christmas-tree-lighting celebration, working with the Make-A-Wish Foundation, which arranges special events for seriously ill children." During the months when no snow falls in south-central Pennsylvania, the Craumers are kept busy with carriage rides for weddings, proms, anniversaries, and other special occasions. Although spring tends to be the slow season in this business, there are occasional bookings for special birthday or anniversary parties, and the decreased business gives the Craumers a chance to prepare for the busy summer months.

Acquiring and maintaining the equipment needed for a horse-drawn carriage business is both expensive and time-consuming. The carriage and harness fittings, as well as the horses themselves, must be positively gleaming, and the driver and assistant dress in formal attire to complete the elegant look people expect when the carriage ride is the centerpiece of a very special event. Like most successful horse careers, the Craumers' business requires a lot of hard work and personal sacrifice. The downside, says Tina, is "mostly just inconsiderate people who don't have any idea of what a horse is." Often people who have not spent much time around horses have no idea how timid and easily frightened the huge animals can be. For a horse, a bit of paper blowing in the breeze or a child pushing a toy truck along the ground can seem as threatening as a hungry lion, and a frightened horse's first instinct is to run away.

"As good as the Percherons are, certain situations, like a parade with loud bands and firecrackers, can set them off and turn into a dangerous scene. You really need two people to do it, and it has to be teamwork—one to drive and one on the ground to work with the horse and any crowd that's around. The ground person has to be someone who knows horses, and who's very sensitive to what the horse is feeling, because the ground person can see the horse's expression, while the driver can't." That's where Tina's husband, whom she describes as a quiet, laid-back man who enjoys both the driving and helping to make an event extra-special for the customer, comes in. Although both Craumers drive the team on occasion, Tina feels especially confident when her husband is helping from the ground. Another major discomfort of the carriage business, Tina points out, is having to work in weather that is far from ideal—say 10 degrees and icy, or 96 degrees and humid, or in a sudden summer thunderstorm. But Tina says that the negatives are far outweighed by the positive side of their thriving business.

"We've met so many people, from all walks of life, through this carriage business. That's a big change in our lives. We can be together as a family, and we get to be outside working with these wonderful animals." Tina and her husband are currently looking for a second Percheron to match Joey, the horse they are now using, and they are thinking of using two of their home-bred quarter horses as a carriage team as well. Eventually, when the children are older and no longer showing the quarter horses, the Craumers hope to begin breeding Percherons as a second business.

Small, family-owned carriage services such as the Craumers' are becoming more common, especially in resort areas and anywhere people want to experience a bit of nostalgia and elegance amid the

Anatomy of a Horse

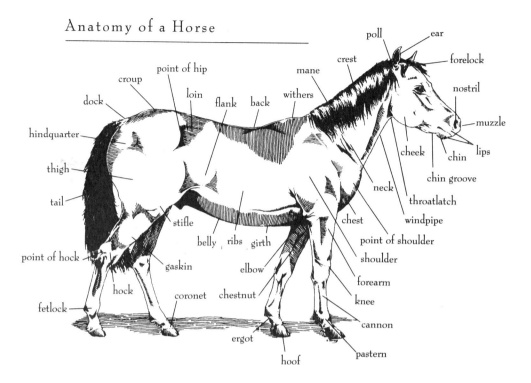

hustle-bustle of modern life. The rapid success of Craumer's Carriage Company proves there is a market for this type of enterprise anywhere, but Tina cautions that location is very important. A business like the Craumers' located in a popular tourist area may earn up to $100,000 a year, but without the tourist trade profits will be more modest. Tina's earnings are currently more in the range of $10,000 to $15,000. She estimates it costs about $200 per month to provide feed and other necessities for the carriage horses, and says that anyone wanting to start a similar business must first have the interest and a lot of commitment, because it is hard work. Although her basic rate for a one-hour carriage ride for a wedding or other event is $350, that one-hour assignment can take about four to six hours of preparation time, including bathing and clipping the horses, cleaning the carriage, preparing clothing, and so on. It takes a lot of basic horse knowledge, too, because a carriage team is not a machine but a pair of living, breathing equines who have the same basic needs as any living being, and the same instincts that all horses share.

A person knowledgeable about horses can learn driving techniques in a number of ways. The American Driving Association may be able to direct you to instruction in your area, either through one of several driving schools throughout the country or through a carriage manufacturer or private instructor. The main requirement is perseverance, says Tina.

"When I see kids who are struggling to learn about horses, and people tell them you can't make any money working with horses, I have to tell them it's just not true. I started at the bottom, with no showing or lessons at all, but I stuck with it, and now it's a business I love."

4

Joan Detlefsen

Equine Musculoskeletal Therapist

THE BIG THOROUGHBRED gelding watches tensely as a small, thin, middle-aged woman begins to touch his neck and shoulder gently and quietly. The horse holds his head stiffly, slightly raised, as if braced against expected pain. The woman moves with the easy assurance of a lifelong horseperson and the catlike grace of a dancer. The horse's owner watches quietly from a corner of the stall. Although Joan Detlefsen is dwarfed by the big show horse, she exudes strength and purpose as she calmly chats with the owner about the horse's recent performance problems, past medical history, and personality. All the while her hands move steadily over the horse's body, but the owner notices that the hands have scarcely touched her horse's sides. Still, as Joan passes her oiled hands over, but slightly away from, the horse's neck, shoulder, back, and legs, the nervous animal unaccountably begins to relax. His head drops several inches, the tightly bunched muscles seem to uncoil, his ears hang at a relaxed angle, and his eyes even begin to close. The horse sighs deeply. Standing on a small plastic step stool, Joan begins gently massaging the horse's body, beginning at his head and working her way over the poll and crest of the neck and along the still-tense back. As she works and asks questions of the owner, her face seems to register the information she "reads" through her hands.

At a time when Americans are exploring new concepts of "wellness" centers, self-help, and preventative and holistic medicine for themselves, horse owners are increasingly interested in alternative therapies for their horses as well. Acupuncture, chiropractic, homeopathy, massage, and herbal remedies are just a few of the approaches gaining wider acceptance in the horse world, not as a replacement for traditional veterinary care but as complementary therapy. Horse owners appreciate the chance to participate more actively in their horses' care that many of these treatment approaches emphasize, and in many cases the results are impressive. Common to all of these "new" treatments (some, like acupuncture and homeopathy, are really quite old) is a consideration for the whole horse and his total well-being—physical, emotional, nutritional, even cellular.

Joan Detlefsen opened her business, In Tact Equine, in Maryland in 1984. Her goal was to bridge the gap between the veterinarian and the farrier (horseshoer) through massage techniques, and to improve the performance of sport horses: as she puts it, "From excellence to magnificence for the equine athlete." The business was a natural outgrowth of a lifetime of experiences with horses, an early career in business, and a personal commitment to holistic approaches to human and animal health.

Like most women who love horses, Joan began dreaming of them very early, and begged her parents for a horse for years. She took riding lessons, and her parents finally answered her pleas when she was nine. Her gelding lived in a fenced one-acre field in the backyard of her Minnesota home during the summertime, and during the school year boarded with Joan's riding instructor, a native of England who had introduced Pony Club to Minnesota. Joan competed at horse shows and foxhunted for many years.

Twenty years ago, Joan began exploring ways to help two of her own horses who were having severe physical and training problems. One mare, a jumper, had been severely injured in a trailer accident and was recuperating slowly and with difficulty. A young Thoroughbred gelding having difficulty adjusting to life after the racetrack led Joan to look for ways to figure out which of his volatile reactions to retraining were a physical response and which were mental and/or training problems. The seeds of In Tact Equine were planted.

Along the way to her present work, Joan has had many teachers. She has studied the work of Jack Meagher, equine massage therapy pioneer; acupuncture with Dr. Marvin Cain, whose efforts had gained acceptance for the technique within the American Veterinary Medical Association; and the homeopathic medical principles of Dr. Dietrich Wiendieck and others.

In Tact Equine treatments are intended to be beneficial to the horse from the very first treatment. Follow-up sessions may be given, depending on the needs of horse and owner. Every treatment includes muscular and skeletal massage. This may be complemented with electrical equipment such as lasers, pulsed magnetic field pads, micro-current therapy, homeopathic remedies, or dietary supplements. Different types of electrical stimulation to various parts of the horse's body can relieve pain, relax muscles and tendons, and help restore mineral balance in the cells, Joan says. Treatments are tailored to the individual horse, and many owners report improved health and enhanced athletic performance.

Like many horsepeople, Joan starts her day early. After taking care of chores in her office, home, and barn, she generally travels to clients' barns to do about two treatments a day. Every six weeks she travels to North Carolina and Virginia, performing three or four treatments a

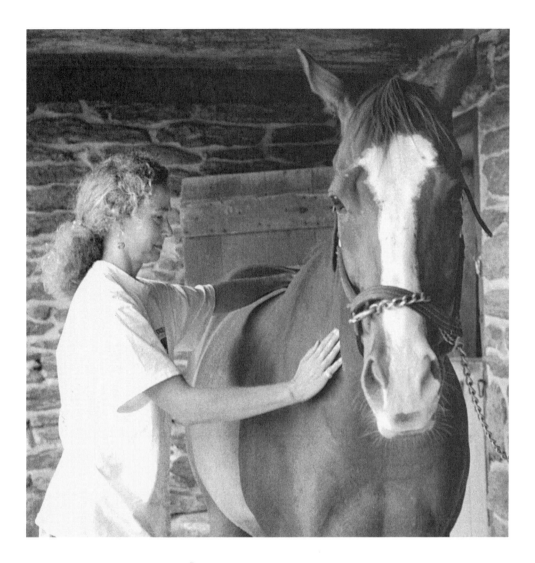

day while away from home. Sometimes she travels as far as Florida to work with hunters and jumpers on the show circuit. When not traveling, she takes care of her farm, her animals, and office correspondence, and tries to ride three days a week. Any other time is reserved for study and research, and teaching some of the principles of her work to other horsepeople.

"I'm headed toward concentrating more on analyzing urine and saliva samples of horses to balance the pH, carbohydrates, and minerals," says Joan. Nutrition therapy is crucial, she believes, and adds,

"You can't guess at it, or just listen to the claims of people who are marketing products." Recently she has begun studying the science and practice of biological agriculture and soil analysis to improve the diets of her clients' horses. Overused or contaminated soils can result in hay and grain that lack nutrients a horse needs to perform at his best, and by testing the soil and the feed for these deficiencies it's possible to make up for lacking minerals and vitamins with feed supplements. By testing urine and saliva samples of horses, and working with laboratory professionals, Joan is able to better determine any nutritional deficiencies an animal may have that can interfere with his body's ability to build energy.

Most of her clients are trainers, who may suggest that their riding students work with Joan, and she has always worked well with veterinarians. Sometimes a client will choose to work with Joan before seeking veterinary treatment, but more often she is consulted after the vet has tried conventional treatments with limited success.

Many of the different aspects of Joan's work lend themselves to potential careers. Massage therapy is an expanding field, and those interested in the health professions may be interested in pursuing acupuncture or homeopathy for horses. A good place to start would be the study of physical therapy and exercise physiology. The field is so new that creating a career in this area is like entering uncharted territory, but Joan has been earning a comfortable income (about $40,000 a year) for a number of years, doing work she loves.

"I don't feel like I've 'arrived,'" she says, "but I have compiled a lot of knowledge and a system that is successful. Eight years ago, nobody was listening to this stuff, it was considered so weird. But now, as more and more vets are getting involved in holistic medicine, it's brought changes in what I'm doing." Nutritional therapy and teaching are areas of her practice that Joan is expanding. As far as she is concerned, the learning never stops, and the possibilities are endless.

5

Joyce Sheppard
Mounted Police Officer

S O M E   W O M E N   S E E M almost to be born on horseback. Horses are their lives from early childhood, when family circumstances or chance and attraction to the animal converge. Others spend their growing-up years dreaming of horses, hoping and planning for the day their dream can become reality. But many come to the dream later in life, and some discover a passion for horses almost by accident. Joyce Sheppard is one of these women. Today her livelihood—and even her life itself—depends on a horse, but until 1985 she had never ridden or associated with any animal larger than a big dog. She wasn't a child with a case of the "horse fever" so many horsewomen report, but what Joyce does admit to is a love of adventure, excitement, and challenge. Joyce is a mounted police officer in Baltimore, Maryland, a bustling city of over 700,000 near the Chesapeake Bay. Baltimore is a beautiful, lively, and cultural city, but a city, like most, with its share of violent crime, poverty, and drugs. It is Joyce Sheppard's hometown, and she has been on its police force for more than a dozen years. But when she first decided to make a career of police work, the image of herself working from the back of a horse was something that had never occurred to her. Now she wouldn't have it any other way.

Joyce's first assignment after graduation from the police academy was regular street patrol, followed by a three-year beat at the city's revitalized inner harbor, a major center of tourism and commerce. By that time, she felt ready for new challenges, so she applied and was accepted for a spot on the force's QRT (Quick Response Team), an elite unit trained to respond to potentially violent situations like hostage-taking. Although this was particularly dangerous work, Joyce loved the excitement, the challenge, and the variety. So did a fellow officer in the unit who was to become her husband. Police regulations forbid a married couple to work in the same unit, though, so in 1985 Joyce applied for a much-sought-after opening in the mounted force when the chief of the unit began to expand and diversify the mounted police. At the time, mounted officers had been largely decorative, spending most of their time writing parking tickets in select city areas, but the new plan was to place mounted police in crime-ridden neighborhoods, allowing them to take advantage of their unique method of transportation in serious tactical work. With her experience on the Quick Response Team, Joyce had the background that was required for these new responsibilities.

Training for mounted patrol work is intense. In only eight weeks, an adult who may have never been near a horse before must not only learn riding fundamentals, but also how to deal with riding in circumstances that would cause many lifelong horsepeople to shudder in horror. "We spent the first six weeks learning to ride in a local city park," says Joyce. The instructor was one of the senior mounted officers, the only one on the force who happens to be a lifelong horseman, with experience as an owner of racehorses and show Arabians. Another of her teachers was a thirty-year veteran of the mounted force, whose own teacher had had years of riding experience rather than any formal instruction.

"The first two weeks of riding were all spent bareback," she remembers, but says that is no longer the case. She nursed some very sore muscles at first, but she learned to stay on, and she learned to begin anticipating the movement of her horse. After six weeks of riding instruction and practice, the rookies were assigned to a two-week training period on the street with an experienced mounted officer. Police riding may lack sophistication and polish, although all of the mounted officers strive to improve their riding all the time. Annual equestrian competitions that draw mounted police from all over the region encourage improved equitation, but what every mounted officer must master first, says Joyce, is to "stay on when the tractor-trailers come by."

Like police officers who work with specially trained dogs, mounted police develop a unique bond with their horses. This bond may be unmatched by professionals and polished amateur riders who ride for profit or sport, since for mounted officers the claim "My horse saved my life that time" may be entirely true.

A new officer in the unit is paired with a horse, sometimes trying several if they are available, until a good match is found. All of the horses on the force are donations, though, and those are hard to come by. The animals must be sound and saddle-broken, at least 15.2 hands tall, and preferably geldings. Naturally a good temperament is crucial, and all potential donations go through a sixty-day trial period to determine if they are suited to police work. There are no breed requirements, and the former preference for dark-colored horses has been relaxed in favor of good horses, whatever the color. The reality, though, according to Joyce, is that "if the horse isn't totally berserk, we usually wind up keeping him. What usually happens is that a horse is paired up with an officer, and that officer winds up falling in love with that particular horse. When that happens, you'll do almost anything to make it work." That's what happened to her. The little chestnut quarter horse had been a show horse in his former life. He was professionally trained but "petrified of the street," Joyce remembers.

"He would rear straight up whenever he saw a truck, and then start tossing his head, trying to get the rider off. The officer who was teamed up with him was an older man who hadn't ridden before, and the horse just kept rearing with him. One time he reared next to a tall truck, and the officer was able to grab on to the scaffolding on the truck and jump off before he fell off. That did it for him; he gave up the horse and left the mounted unit." Joyce was then given the horse, and he continued to rear whenever the street traffic rattled him. But Joyce was determined.

"You have this macho thing drilled into you during training. You never get off your horse, no matter how scared you are. And you never ride back into the barn, because you know you'll never live it down." So Joyce never got off, and she never fell off, and eventually the little horse adjusted to city life and stopped rebelling. "He turned out to be the best horse we had," says Joyce. "Everyone wanted to ride him." Recently retired at age sixteen due to a soundness problem, the horse is a pet now. He was given to Joyce, and she boards him near her home. Retiring police horses are always offered to their riders first, if they can provide proper facilities for the animals' care. If not, they are given to another officer through a lottery system, and all are provided a comfortable retirement. When her horse was retired Joyce was on maternity leave for the birth of her fourth child, but soon she'll be starting over with a new horse.

The mounted unit horses are housed in a barn/barracks building in the heart of Baltimore. Their care, feeding, and grooming are provided for around the clock. On a typical day, Joyce first reports for

roll call and is given her assignment for the day, usually in a high-crime area. Officers are briefed on what the predominant crime problems are in the neighborhood, and then they tack up their horses and ride out to the location assigned, usually in pairs, although sometimes four officers may be assigned to one area. On the street they work a regular beat, sometimes stopping cars and giving out moving violations. "People wonder how we can do that," says Joyce with a laugh, "but in the city traffic doesn't move that fast, and they always have to stop at the next light." Whatever comes up, the mounted officer deals with it, whether it is a burglary or a drug bust. Mounted officers carry city-wide radios and can travel to any nearby area where they may be needed.

You have to love this work. As a civil service job, the pay is relatively modest for the demands of the work, although it varies depending on location. Mounted officers earn the same salary as other police officers, and in the city of Baltimore, where Joyce works, starting pay is $28,000, climbing to a top salary of $33,000 after five years. But in nearby, more affluent Prince Georges County, Maryland, officers start at $46,000 per year. And in police work everywhere, while many days are routine, the element of danger is always present.

"The thing we do most is drug busts," says Joyce. "We've had to hide in alleys, and then ride out quickly and surprise the drug dealers. I've been shot at, and we've had to get guns off of guys many times." Besides the courage, judgment, and quick reactions required of anyone who wants to do police work, the main prerequisite for a mounted officer, says Joyce, is "the love of the horse. You have to really want to ride, even when it's freezing cold. But then you get the beautiful sunny days, too. I just love the work, and I love riding. Lots of people pay to do this." Of course, most of those people don't routinely get shot at during their rides. But, says Joyce, "This is something you either love or you don't. It comes to you right away, and you know it's going to be fun." Despite the risks and discomforts, every time there is an opening on the unit, close to a hundred officers apply.

Most days a mounted officer will be in the saddle at least six hours, with fifteen-minute breaks every hour, plus lunch. "A lot of people can't take sitting on their butts that long," says Joyce, but the new padded Australian saddles the force bought has helped. And like many people for whom riding is their work, Joyce never rides on her days off. "Maybe if my husband and I could do it together without feeling guilty about leaving the children, then it would be fun. But at this point, that's not possible." She plans to stay with the mounted unit, though. The love of horses is persistent, and now she can't imagine living or working without them.

6

Teresa Vanderlaan
Equine Photographer

INVENTING A CAREER with horses is often a matter of combining other interests with an equine background. When you discover what challenges you, what you know how to do or want to learn, you'll often find that a seemingly unrelated skill can complement your love of horses perfectly. That's what Teresa Vanderlaan did when she combined a lifelong association with horses with an interest in photography, becoming an equine photographer.

Horses have been a favorite subject for artists since the Stone Age, and a walk through any bookstore will reveal that the animal holds a special appeal for photographic artists. For many, the horse epitomizes beauty, grace, strength, and freedom of spirit, so it's no wonder the equine form is displayed on so many large, glossy books, posters, and calendars. When the first prototype of the modern camera was developed in 1816, horses became a favorite subject of photographers, despite the frustrations of getting an impatient horse to stand perfectly still for the extended exposure time needed to make a da-

guerreotype in the old days. Daguerreotypes were an early type of
photograph in which the image was made on a light-sensitive silver-
coated metallic plate, a process that was much slower than the way
images are created on modern film with the click of a shutter. Even
with modern 35-millimeter cameras and fast film and shutter speeds,
horses are difficult to photograph well. It is almost imperative that a
photographer of horses be an experienced horseperson. Understanding how horses think, move, and react will increase the chances of
being able to coax them into a desirable but natural pose. And knowing what is the most important moment in a competitive event will
make it possible to click the shutter at the right time and from the
best angle.

Now in her early thirties, Teresa can't remember a time when
horses weren't a part of her life. Until she was six, her family lived in
Vermont, where her mother kept Arabians. Then the family moved

to Nashville, Tennessee, where Teresa joined the local Pony Club and rode both hunters and event horses. At an early age she was helping to start young horses in training and prepare them for sale. By the time she was twelve, the family had moved again.

"Horses remained a major part of my life through my school years," she says, "even though we were moving a lot and I didn't always have access to them." In 1981, at the age of eighteen, Teresa moved to Lexington, Kentucky, to work for a racehorse breeding farm. She soon became very involved in the racing industry, first in breeding, then selling, and later as a buying agent. But after years of working in an industry that was suffering a serious recession, she became discouraged and felt she needed to take a different direction with her career.

In 1985 Teresa became interested in photography. "I bought a cheap 35-millimeter camera and took some classes. I started taking a lot of shots around town and at the horse sales and other events. When I showed the results to my friends I got a lot of positive feedback and encouragement, so I bought a better camera, took some more classes, and started to sell some of my photos to grooms, buyers, and sellers. By 1988 I was getting calls to do photos for people on commission, and I realized it was time I started taking photography more seriously as a business." In 1989 she decided to move to Los Angeles, establishing herself as a full-time photographer with her base around the southern California racetracks. "I found that I enjoyed taking 'art' photos and selling a finished framed photo, as well as doing commissioned portraits."

The next year saw another move, this time to the Philadelphia area, where Teresa moved onto a farm and, she says, "finally settled down." Photography is a part-time business for now, as she is also busy taking care of a variety of animals on the farm. Besides the three horses, there are sheep, pigs, cows, and cats. She also does some modeling and acting, but equine photography continues to be an active career that also provides the flexibility she needs. It is a field with possibilities limited only by talent and imagination, in which an understanding of horses and horsemen is as important as photographic technique. Lifelong horsewoman Alix Coleman of nearby Bryn Mawr, Pennsylvania, for example, is an internationally recognized equine photographer whose work has appeared in seventeen books and many magazines, and who credits much of her success to her background in dressage as well as her training as a painter.

Teresa currently does photos of stallions and show horses for advertising purposes and also photographs horse-show competitors. "I enjoy selling my photos as art," she says, "and now I'm working on hand-coloring techniques for black-and-white photos."

There are a number of ways to acquire the technical skills required to build a career as a horse photographer. Most local colleges and art schools offer basic photography courses, which cover equipment and basic principles of shooting and processing film as well as composition. But a university degree is not necessary to succeed in equine photography. Local camera clubs and art leagues may be another source of instruction, or even home study (correspondence) courses, which are often advertised in photography magazines. Possibly one of the best ways to learn is by arranging an apprenticeship with an experienced photographer, if you know someone in the business or can find someone through other contacts. Since there are no schools that specialize in teaching how to take a good portrait of a horse, the only other way to learn the specifics of good equine photography is to look at pictures that successful photographers have taken. By studying good examples of the art in detail and analyzing the choices the artist has made in terms of the pose of the animal, background, camera angle, cropping, and so forth, you can begin to get a feeling for what makes a good horse portrait or action shot.

Once you've mastered the fundamentals and acquired a camera and a few basic lenses, Teresa says the best way to learn is to "take lots of pictures and develop your eye for details. Always make sure your photos are very sharp and properly printed." The technical side of photography can be learned by anyone willing to spend the time working at it, but having an eye for a photograph is something else. Like any creative skill, the ability to compose beautiful, effective, and dramatic photos just seems to come naturally to some people. The only way to find out if you are one of them, and to begin to develop your ability, is to shoot hundreds and hundreds of pictures, in as many different settings and lighting situations as you can find.

Attention to detail means taking the utmost care to present the subject in the most flattering or accurate (depending on the purpose of the assignment) light possible. This means insistence on proper lighting conditions and background, thorough grooming of the horse, and perfect timing for action shots. It also means taking many more photographs than you will use; you may shoot ten rolls of film to get that one perfect shot. Many equine photographers specialize in a particular breed or discipline, photographing just quarter horses or Arabians, or concentrating on the racetrack or the hunter circuit, for example. The reason for this is simple: each breed or discipline exhibits special conformation traits or desirable form, and it's up to the photographer to play up these aspects of their subjects. So the successful photographer must be thoroughly familiar with her subject, both breed and discipline. Beyond that, a good portrait photographer will try to analyze and capture the personality of her equine subject.

Besides technical and artistic skills, you'll also need to consider marketing your work. "A lot of the horse magazines and newsletters accept photos every month from freelance photographers and will pay for any photos that they use." There are also stock photo agencies that may agree to market your work for a percentage of the sales; the advantage is that you will likely make far more sales that way than you could on your own. With commission portraits and possibly regular work at horse shows involving direct sales to owners and riders, a good horse photographer can put together a pretty good income. Teresa's rates vary, depending on the type of assignment she is working on. If she travels to a farm to shoot a conformation photo, she charges a set rate of $50 per roll of film she shoots, with a minimum of three rolls. If the owner then purchases an eight-by-ten print, there is an additional charge of $20 per print. If Teresa is photographing individual competitors at a horse show, she offers prints to the owners at $15 to $40 per print, depending on the size of the print and whether it is black-and-white or color. For magazine work, she says, you have to plan to shoot a lot of film, but you'll only get paid for what the magazine uses, so you might make anywhere from $20 to $400 per day, minus your expenses.

"You have to like the work," says Teresa. "It has to be fun. But you can certainly make a comfortable living at it." For a horse photographer working full-time, it's reasonable to expect an income of about $30,000 to $40,000 per year if, says Teresa, you're willing to work hard and really hustle.

"If one is tenacious," says Teresa, "one can make a living, meet a lot of people, and have a lot of fun at all of the horse shows and events." Teresa, like many other successful equine photographers, has maintained her personal contact with the world of competitive riding. She's competing in three-day events with her preliminary-level horse, as time permits. "Horses have always been the focus of both fun and work for me," she says.

7

Cindy Halle
Polo Coach

IT'S A FREEZING NIGHT in late November, and it's not much warmer in the tiny, unheated tackroom tucked into the back of a barn at Garrison Forest School in suburban Baltimore, Maryland. Cindy Halle's fingers are so cold that she's having trouble with the buckles on the stiff bridles she's adjusting for tonight's class, six enthusiastic adult polo students who will soon arrive to help tack up the polo lesson ponies. She's glad she already has on warm leather chaps over her jeans, thick wool socks under her boots, and her heavy barn jacket, but still, she'll be happy to get this lesson started so she can warm up. Teaching this sport in the winter still seems strange, since polo is a summer game, usually filled with excitement and sweat, white-garbed players and hot ponies darting across expanses of green grass, tailgate lunches, and spectators in straw hats and sundresses. But though Cindy plays amateur polo with the local club every summer, her job is to teach teenage girls the sport during the other nine months of the year. And because so many adults in the community are interested in learning the game, she also has a class for both men and women one night a week. Her adult students are passionate about polo. They have to be, to come out on a night like this.

Tonight there's a new pony to work with, a lovely bay Thoroughbred recently retired from the show ring. As the lesson starts, the gelding is nervous in the cold air of the indoor arena, spooking at the sounds echoing off the walls, prancing away from the steady old quarter horses and crossbreds on which Cindy's students are mounted. Cindy is riding the Thoroughbred, trying to be as soft and tactful as she can to help him get used to his new surroundings and job, while still shouting out instructions and encouragement to her class. The first exercise is to take the ball down the center of the arena, with each student getting a turn to practice taking it away from his opponent. Working in pairs, the students canter slowly down the center line at Cindy's signal, concentrating on correct body position, proper control of the mallet, and safe, effective positioning of the pony. Timing is everything, and it takes most of the students a few tries before they begin to get it. Even though she is considered one of the top female polo players in the country, Cindy can still remember, when she was first learning the game more than a decade ago, how awkward it felt to swing the mallet and ride in a straight line at the same time.

You might think polo is a sport reserved for the princes and dukes of Europe, but for Cindy it has been a way of life since her teen years. She began riding at age ten, but it was years before she owned a horse. Instead, she was a working student, doing barn chores to help pay for her lessons, and "catch riding" other people's horses at local horse shows.

"I hated it then," says Cindy, "because I could hardly ever win, since I was always riding difficult horses. But I'm glad now, because I learned so much more that way." For years she asked her parents for a horse of her own. Instead, she remembers, "I got a puppy." Undaunted, she eventually bred the Labrador retriever, sold the puppies, and was finally able to buy herself a horse, a quarter horse/Paint cross that she went on to show successfully. But then, when Cindy was in high school, her trainer moved out of the area. At about that time, she learned that a local man needed someone to exercise his polo ponies, so she took the job simply because it offered another opportunity to earn money riding.

"I got curious about the game then," she says, "and after I graduated I enrolled at the University of California at Davis, which was the only college in the state with a polo club. A lot of the people I played with in college are now pros." After graduating with a degree in animal science, she began working as an equine surgical nurse at the UC/Davis teaching hospital. It was when she was asked to teach a lab in bandaging techniques to undergraduates that Cindy discovered how much she enjoyed teaching and working with younger students.

As a student at UC/Davis Cindy played on four national championship teams, serving as cocaptain on the last two. Today, at age thirty-one, she is one of the most respected woman players in the United States, and has won several major tournaments. Her prominence in what was still a little-known sport in this country led to an offer in 1986 to help organize a polo team at Garrison Forest School, a girls' preparatory school in suburban Baltimore. The West Coast native traveled east to talk with school officials, fell in love with the area and the school (as well as with Ned Halle, attorney, farmer, avid foxhunter, and the man who would become her husband), and became Garrison Forest's first full-time polo coach.

What does she like the most about her job? That's easy, says Cindy. It's the kids. "It's never routine," she says. "Dealing with kids on a day-to-day basis is never boring." A typical day's work may entail overseeing the care of a colicky pony, evaluating a potential donation horse as a polo school prospect, counseling a student on a problem in her personal life, tinkering with a temperamental tractor before dragging a harrow over the riding arena, sweeping up the barn, moving heavy equipment, umpiring a practice game, and hopping on a green polo pony to demonstrate a particular skill of the game to a group of students. As a horsewoman, she needs to know how to keep her equine athletes healthy and fit, and how to evaluate and give first aid for any injuries that may occur during a rough game. As a teacher, she must relate to fellow faculty and staff at the school as well as to her students, who range from middle school age to the adult beginners who make up Cindy's weekly "open" class.

From September until June, Cindy coaches approximately fifteen teenage girls who participate in polo much as they would in any other varsity sport. What sets Cindy apart from other varsity coaches, of course, is that she is the coach of rider and pony *together*. Students come to the polo program having already mastered basic riding skills, but Cindy must impart the very specialized requirements of the sport, a fast, rough game whose rules are largely designed to ensure safety for riders and ponies.

Polo has exploded in popularity in America over the past decade, resulting in a 50-percent increase in the number of club and individual memberships in the United States Polo Association. Spectators are fascinated by the sport's explosive action, its intricate timing and accuracy, and the all-important relationship between horse and rider. They also appreciate the pleasant surroundings in which polo is played: a green playing field 300 yards long and 160 yards wide—ten acres (the size of ten football fields put together)—manicured like a golf course to help the ball go fast. They like it when spectators are invited onto the field to replace the divots of turf churned up by ten 1,200-pound Thoroughbreds galloping at up to forty miles per hour, pounding the grass with their hooves, cutting right or left or skidding to a halt. Players love the speed, precision, and unpredictability of the game. And, of course, the horses.

Garrison Forest School polo team members play teams from other high school programs around the country, with a national high school–level tournament held annually. Cindy is proud that her kids won the women's interscholastic title in 1992. Because there are still relatively few high school clubs, the Garrison Forest girls also play college clubs on an informal basis, as a learning experience. Last year the team competed with Georgetown, the University of Virginia, Cornell, Yale, Skidmore, Harvard, and Pace University, among others.

"Some of the kids can even use polo to help them get into colleges," said Cindy. "It's a club sport, not an NCAA [National Collegiate Athletic Association] sport, but there are enough college programs that about a third of my girls go on to play at college. And whether they do or not, all of them gain a lot of confidence and have a lot of fun, playing to the level of men and people older than themselves. My girls don't get intimidated easily."

The four-legged members of Cindy's team, called "ponies" in polo jargon even though they are actually horses, are all either donated or loaned to the school, and many are so experienced that Cindy almost thinks of them as assistant coaches. Most are older animals, at least fifteen and some as old as twenty-five. Cindy says that the best polo ponies are Thoroughbreds from Mexico and Argentina that are bred especially for the game, but quarter horses crossed with Thoroughbreds also excel, especially as school ponies.

During the school year, Cindy puts in about twenty-five to thirty hours a week at her job. With her own farm (about twenty horses at home) and a small daughter to care for, it's a very active life. During the summer season she plays amateur polo with the local club, and in the fall and winter she sometimes joins husband Ned in foxhunting. Horses are a big part of her life year-round.

"Polo still has a glamour, elitist image," says Cindy, "but today it's also possible for regular middle-class people to play. Club and local polo can be played with two horses, a trailer, and no groom, to start." She says that as polo clubs spring up in communities and schools around the nation, there are many more opportunities for instructing positions. Some programs are run by volunteers, but paid coaching positions offer salaries in the range of $12,000 to $24,000 per year. "People are starting to realize how important it is to have a coach." It's a unique kind of teaching, like being a riding instructor but with the additional demands of team dynamics. And because teams are small, just four players on the field at a time, interpersonal relationships become very important.

If you want to be a polo coach, you need to be a player first. One way to start is by offering to groom for an experienced player. If there is a club or lesson program in your area, you can begin learning there. Information on clinics, clubs, and lessons is available through the United States Polo Association, and you might want to consider subscribing to *Polo* magazine, the official voice of American polo. You never know. As Cindy Halle will tell you, a chance encounter with polo just might change your life.

8

Andrea Seefeldt

Jockey

WHEN ANDREA SEEFELDT first came to the racetrack, still in high school, her plan was to earn enough money to support her expensive weekend hobby—showing junior jumpers at American Horse Shows Association–recognized shows. "Within three weeks, I had sold the show horses," she says without a touch of regret. "I knew what I wanted to do. I told everyone I wanted to be a jockey when I grew up." Now, more than a decade later, Andrea is approaching her own self-imposed deadline for retiring from the sport—age thirty. But the last couple of years have been her best ever, and she admits that "riding is hard to give up. It gets in your blood." And if things keep going as well as they have, she may keep riding for a lot longer than she had planned. She finished 1992 as the seventh-ranking female jockey in the nation, based on purses earned (403 women are licensed in the U.S.; there are currently 2,100 licensed male jockeys), the only female jockey riding on a daily basis in Maryland, and one of only two jockeys in the state who handle their own business affairs.

The year before, Andrea became the third female in the 117-year history of the Kentucky Derby to ride in the fabled race at Churchill Downs, aboard Forty Something. She won the Pennsylvania Derby on Valley Crossing, becoming the first female jockey ever to win one of the twenty-six derbys run in America annually, and also rode in Japan in the International Female Jockey Challenge, winning two of the fourteen races. It looked like 1991 would be the best year ever for her until a nasty fall in November resulted in a compound fracture of her collarbone, putting her out of action until well into 1992. That was only the latest in a string of injuries that have punctuated her career in this most dangerous of sports, but she sees a positive side to all that: "Every time I have been hurt," she says, "I've come back to do better than ever."

Andrea says she fell in love with horses at the age of three, and her first mount was "a stick horse I rode all over the house. I rode my first real horse at summer camp when I was six, and started tak-

ing English riding lessons at eight." By the time she was ten Andrea got her first pony and began going to 4-H shows along with her older brother, Paul. Gradually the pair moved up to better shows and more expensive horses, and when Paul got a job at nearby Bowie racetrack to help pay for the show horses, Andrea followed. Her first job as a hot walker at age fifteen eventually led to grooming and then exercise riding.

"It was very hard to get anybody to take me seriously at first, to let me gallop the horses. In 1980 there were very few successful female jockeys or even exercise riders. You have to work as an exercise rider for at least a year, and preferably two or three years, before you can become a jockey. It is very hard, and very different from any other type of horseback riding I'd ever done. So it's very risky, from the trainer's point of view, to let an inexperienced rider get on these valuable but high-strung horses (the cheapest racehorse in Maryland, for example, is worth $5,000).

"After almost two years of walking hots and then grooming, I finally found someone to give me a chance. I groomed five horses and he let me get on one very quiet horse a day. After that I got a job as an exercise rider, and I rode my first race in May of 1981 at Pimlico, finishing second." Although Andrea is tall for a jockey at five feet, six and a half inches, she is very thin, careful to maintain her weight at no more than 111 or 112 pounds. Brother Paul, who is tall and, at 150 pounds, well over the weight limit for a jockey, had to settle for becoming a trainer of racehorses instead. It was Paul who gave Andrea her first mount on her way back from what might have been a career-ending injury—a shattered pelvis from a starting-gate accident with a three-year-old filly she was schooling. The horse panicked on that frosty January morning, ran backward out of the gate, and fell on her jockey. By May Andrea was back in the saddle, winning her first race on Ivory Coast, a four-year-old filly trained by her brother.

"Before that, I was having some doubts about whether this was really what I should be doing," she says. "But after that race there was no question. To me, riding is everything, and winning a race makes you forget about everything bad that happens."

Although it is exciting, being a jockey consists of more hard work than glamour. Says Andrea: "I get up at 5:00 A.M. every day except Sunday and go straight to the track [Pimlico Race Track, in Baltimore] to 'work' or breeze horses. From six to ten, the track is open for training, and on a typical day I'll work one horse for a trainer, then go to the next trainer and work another. I line up my upcoming mounts with the trainer while I'm there, which would be my agent's job if I had one." Andrea had to learn to be her own agent in the early years of her career, when she wasn't getting enough good mounts to be attractive to a professional agent, and now, she says, "Most trainers ride me because of me, not because of an agent, so I'm better off working by myself." But hustling for mounts adds hours to her working day. "I ride for one twenty-five-horse outfit, and twenty-five one-horse outfits, and I need to stop and check with every one of them every day. If you work a horse, then you are supposed to get to ride it when it races, but we don't get paid for the morning work."

By 11:00 A.M., she must be in the jockeys' room at the track, waiting for her races, and she is not allowed to leave until after her last race. Since Andrea usually rides in three or four races each day, she often winds up being at the track from the first to the last race of the day. Then she goes home, except that at least a couple of times a week she has mounts to ride at another track where there is night racing. On those nights she drives straight from Pimlico to the other track in Pennsylvania, New York, or New Jersey and follows the same procedure there, finally getting home sometime between 11:00 P.M. and 2:00 A.M. At five the next morning, it starts all over again. Sometimes a trainer will ship one of her regular mounts to another track out of

Maryland for a better race, and Andrea will travel there to ride the horse, giving her other mounts at the home track to someone else to ride that day.

"The easy part is riding the race," Andrea insists. "The hard part is getting the mounts and keeping the mounts." It's especially hard for a woman, who faces a lot of prejudice on the part of some trainers. Sometimes it seems as if a woman jockey must be twice as good as a man to be considered half as good. There's a lot more to riding a racehorse than strength, although physical strength is important. Communication with the horse is just as important, and Andrea says that a real rider is someone who can sense what kind of ride that particular horse needs to run his best. Sometimes the jockey will not have ridden the horse before she enters the starting gate, and instructions from the trainer may be minimal, so judgment and lightning-quick reactions are everything.

Andrea's strengths as a rider may stem from spending all those childhood years with all kinds of horses, from the stick pony on up. "I'm patient, and I'm kind to horses," she says, "because I like them, and they respond well to me. I have developed a reputation as a closing rider, but I feel like I ride just as well in front as I do from behind. I always save something for the end no matter where I am. I get my horses to relax, and I have perseverance."

It is the horse that makes a jockey successful, but the more a jockey wins, the better her chances of getting better mounts in the future. Luck enters into the equation, but a successful rider has to have the skill to take advantage of any lucky breaks. And although the possibility of serious injury is something all jockeys acknowledge, Andrea says you can't dwell on it if you want to ride. Although catastrophic injuries are fortunately infrequent, everyday lumps and bumps, aches and pains are something every jockey lives with. Collisions with the starting gate are routine, and a jockey's soft boot is designed more for a sensitive feel of the horse than for protection. Once out of the gate, the jockey must not only stay on a barely broken half-ton animal careening at forty miles per hour, perched over the horse's shoulder with only her balance to keep her on, but she has to keep her excited mount absolutely straight to avoid interfering with other horses and possibly causing a collision. Sometimes a horse goes down in a race and the jockey takes a hard fall. Although he or she is "uninjured" and comes back to ride in the next race, the fact is that the jockey will be bruised and sore for days. "But," says Andrea simply, "you ride if you can."

Like many bruising, high-risk sports, riding racehorses can be very lucrative when a jockey is successful. In 1992 Andrea earned over a million dollars in purses, of which the jockey's share is 10 percent. There are no guarantees, though.

There is very little time for any kind of social life outside the track, but that doesn't bother someone who loves the life. A few years ago Andrea gave up riding to be married. She worked as a secretary, but the marriage didn't last, and in less than two years she was back at the track. The racetrack community is a kind of society within itself, says Andrea, with plenty of opportunity for socializing. There's even a track softball league, and lots of people go out together after the softball games. There are no scheduled vacations, of course. "The only vacations you get are when you get hurt."

The only way to get started on the road to being a jockey, says Andrea, is to find a trainer with a good reputation and start at the bottom. Plan to be very patient. "You have to be able to withstand cold, lack of sleep, rejection, pain, more rejection, and more pain." On the other hand, she says, it's worth it. "What can compare with this? You get to be your own boss, you're outside, you see a hundred people a day, and you get to work with these fantastic animals." And thrills? "I used to love roller coasters when I was a kid," says Andrea. "But now I don't enjoy them that much anymore. I get plenty of thrills in my daily life."

9

Sondra Howell

Equestrian Movement Therapist

"SIT UP STRAIGHT! Shoulders back! Heels down!" Anyone who has ever taken a riding lesson has heard these commands countless times. But Sondra Howell, whose practice is called "Body Education for Riders," offers an alternative to the idea that there is one "correct" riding posture for everybody.

"Posture is, above all, movable and natural and not something that needs to be worked at," she says. "Each body is unique in its individual structure or conformation and is unique in how it balances its body mass. The only rule about posture is that it should be an equal distribution, a balance, of tensional forces from within the body that relate to the space surrounding a rider." In other words, how a person's body moves depends on the natural balance and shape of that body, and it is much easier and more comfortable for a person to move in the way that is most natural, instead of following some kind of "ideal" posture or way of moving. Riding is just one way of moving your body through space, and adapting those movements to follow the motion of the horse helps the horse to also move more freely and naturally. Movement theory can be applied to riders as well as dancers, football quarterbacks, or anyone else engaging in an intense and demanding physical activity. But a movement therapist who works with riders must always take into account the movement of the horse's body as well as the rider's.

Sondra has been working with riders and their horses since 1985, when she moved from Philadelphia to the surrounding countryside and began to ride. After she began going to some local horse shows as a spectator, she noticed that almost all the riders she saw were forcing their bodies into a rigid posture. "I began to discover that when my teacher told me to pull my shoulders back, in order to create an upright line, that it didn't feel natural or comfortable, and since my training has been to really 'listen to' my body and work with it in a sensory awareness way, I knew that using a prescribed set of posture 'rules' for everyone would only create a lot of effort and strain."

Sondra has been a body and movement therapist since 1975, and was originally trained as a teacher of the Alexander Technique. Alexander was a turn-of-the-century Tasmanian actor who developed theories of movement to help solve his own speech difficulties. His techniques of body control and visualization are invaluable to musicians, actors, and athletes—people whose very lives revolve around communicating with their bodies.

"These are people who feel stuck in getting their message across," says Sondra. "Nowadays, all sorts of people are beginning to realize that they could have better balance than they now do." Practitioners of the technique are specially trained to analyze a body's movement and then gently repattern that movement as necessary with the hands. Using her hands to manipulate the deep tissue and muscles of the body, the therapist works to help the body find its own most natural position with relation to gravity, and to the demands of the particular type of riding that is the goal. Then, by careful observation of the rider and horse working together, the therapist is able to analyze rider position and movement for imbalances and inefficient posture, which can make every movement difficult and uncomfortable for horse and rider alike. Sometimes the therapist will gently place a rider's thigh or shoulder in the proper position, a position that may at first feel awkward and wrong to a rider who has been trying for years to force her body into a posture that is unnatural for it. The results can be as subtle as a smoother, more polished dressage test or as basic as the difference between falling off and staying in the saddle.

"One of my clients once told me that she had come to an awareness that the reason she fell off her horse going over a jump was because she held her body so tight up there that she was like a clothespin that just popped off. The effort required to maintain 'good posture' did

not allow this rider to interact and flow with the movement of her horse. At the precise moment when she needed to be the most flexible and in contact with her horse's movement, her very unyieldingness literally propelled her from her seat."

Sondra's unusual career requires both a wide range and a depth of knowledge about the way bodies work, as well as an understanding of the special demands placed upon a rider. In addition to training in the Alexander Technique, she studied anatomy and kinesiology (the science of movement), as well as structural therapy, involving massage of the muscles and connective tissues (tendons and ligaments).

Standard training for a registered movement therapist will last about two to three years, and most are in private practice. Sondra travels to her private clients three days a week, in addition to conducting mounted and unmounted Alexander Balanced Riding Clinics. The purpose of her work is to release habitual patterns that control the way people hold their bodies, whether caused by physical structure, injury, emotional state ("nerves"), or simply habit. During a typical therapy session, Sondra will observe a rider's movement, and her trained eye will "read" the body for errors in structural balance and inhibiting movement patterns. She can then use her hands to restructure the rider's posture into a more comfortable and efficient position. This allows the rider to move with the horse in a lighter, more sensitive way and to maintain this new, freer and more relaxed posture with every ride.

Mary Long is a dressage rider who has been working with Sondra for about five years. She says the training has completely changed the way she rides, and made her really enjoy all of her rides. "I was very tense before," she says. "I knew I needed to start over in a different way." Now if her horse is tense or overly energetic, she can ride through a few bucks feeling relaxed and confident, helping the horse to settle and focus on his work.

Releasing the tension in a rider's body usually has dramatic effects on the tension of his or her mount as well. It is impossible to separate rider problems and horse problems. In her work with riders Sondra has noticed a slowly growing awareness that there may be some link between the rider's stiff and frozen neck and the fact that the horse has a stiff neck as well, held high and tense instead of extending in a natural, relaxed manner to help to balance the horse's body.

"The more you impose on your own body, the more you impose on your horse's body," says Sondra. She says that there is a trend for massage therapists with an interest in horses to study and practice horse massage. But although Sondra has expanded her practice to include horses, dogs, and other domestic animals, her focus is on movement rather than massage. "I analyze a horse's movement for restriction, and massage the muscles, joints, and tendons to bring more length and ease to the area. The work is similar for humans, but with people it also includes reeducating the person's habitual neuromuscular patterns. The horse, most times, will naturally move with ease after the restriction is freed up, but the human carries mental and emotional baggage that needs repatterning—worries about how our posture should 'look' and so forth—so we get in the way of our own bodies more than animals do. If a horse postures, or assumes an exaggerated straightness, it happens only because the rider manipulates the horse into doing so. Left to its own intelligence, a horse or any other animal will naturally move with length and expansion."

The field of movement therapy is growing and changing, as more riders and trainers become aware that physical and mental roadblocks are closely linked in both equine and human bodies. In 1985, when Sondra first began working with riders and horses, Sally Swift's popular book, *Centered Riding*, which described how the Alexander Technique could help riders relate to their horses in a whole new way, had just been published. The book helped to lay the groundwork for her,

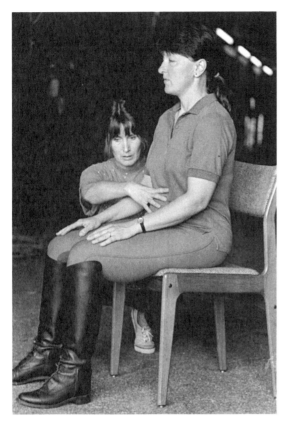

says Sondra, and people who had read it were very receptive and eager to work with someone who could help them put Swift's principles into action. She began to build a clientele by accepting invitations from riding clubs and other organizations to lecture on her ideas and techniques. She also attended conferences with other horsepeople, which provided networking opportunities, and she invested in high-quality promotional materials such as brochures and newsletters with good graphic art and readable type. She spent time analyzing her potential market, obtained mailing lists from horse associations and clubs, and mailed brochures to barns and organizations listed in horse magazines. Some she delivered personally to tack shops and feed stores.

"Within a year of starting," she says, "I had people coming to five or six group clinics I presented during the year. My business is self-selecting, in the sense that riders interested enough in the subject to choose to come to a clinic are already very receptive to my ideas, and don't consider them weird or silly. They are my clients, and I've never really had to try to convince people who are truly skeptical of anything new.

"The whole discipline is being revolutionized," says Sondra, "as the conception of what posture on a horse should be has changed. It's very exciting." What is most rewarding in her work is seeing a real difference in the performance of riders and their horses, whether they are competing more successfully or just enjoying the trails together. Some of her clients are successful competitors in three-day eventing and dressage. Others are simply pleasure riders who want to make their riding experience more pleasurable for them and their horse.

Sondra sees private clients three days a week, spending the balance of her time operating her own farm, where she raises dairy goats and makes cheese. She gives clinics on a regular basis, and is also called upon to give deep muscle therapy to horses and dogs. The dogs may have been referred for rehabilitation after orthopedic surgery, or may be seemingly healthy dogs who have difficulty in obedience training. Most of the horses Sondra sees have been injured or have suffered strains because their riders are interfering with the horse's natural flow of movement.

For anyone truly committed to helping horses and their riders to achieve their full potential, the prospects for success in the field of movement therapy are bright. A full-time practitioner can expect to earn from $25,000 up to $50,000 per year. The requirements are patience and attention to detail, a thorough training program in movement therapy, anatomy, and physiology, and above all, a love for the horse.

10

Amy Donehower
Mobile Tack Shop Owner and Saddler

SOME HORSE ENTHUSIASTS discover their life's work early; for others, years of trial and error finally lead to a satisfying career. For Amy Donehower, carving out a niche in the horse world was a process of discovery, beginning with her own discovery of horses as a ten-year-old Girl Scout growing up in Indiana. She learned to ride at a summer camp for scouts, and although she rode only in the summers, she was soon teaching others at the camp. After a few years, though, a teenage Amy discovered boys and other social attractions, and for about ten years she had no contact with horses whatsoever. She went to college and graduate school, eventually earning a master's degree in social work, and she worked in that field for about four years. It was very stressful work.

"I found I was getting physically sick," Amy remembers, "just totally burned out. I figured I'd better find something else to do." She remembered how happy she had been working with horses years earlier. She decided to try combining her love of riding with her experience in human services by working in the area of therapeutic riding. It didn't take long for her to realize that this wasn't for her, either. After much soul-searching, she decided she'd like to become a riding instructor, but she felt the need for much more formal training than she'd had as a rider. In search of a more complete training program that would give her the basic knowledge she felt she needed to teach others to ride safely and properly, she traveled to England and entered an instructor training program offered by the British Horse Society. She completed the program, received certification as a riding instructor, and returned to the United States to begin teaching, which she did for about three years.

"All this time," says Amy now, "I still felt the need for more training." Even though many riding instructors have had far less formal instruction than she had, she says, "I wasn't comfortable with my level of knowledge and experience." In the United States, most professional riding instructors began their careers as riders, and their teaching credentials are based on that experience, rather than any formal training in how to instruct others to ride.

"I felt that I shouldn't be out there teaching other people to ride because it was too dangerous, and I thought that if I was going to continue teaching, I'd really have to go back to England about every three years to get more training." During this time she was working with an English friend who was designing saddles and importing tack from Europe to sell in the United States.

"She taught me a lot about saddles, and she put me in contact with another friend who was interested in starting a saddlery business." The two formed a partnership in the late summer of 1988, and began taking saddles and supplies around to various barns in their area. This business eventually expanded to include traveling to shows and other equine events with a van loaded with saddles, bridles, and other essential items. In March of 1992, Amy bought out her partner's interest in the business and continued on her own, working the shows, horse trials, and events, as well as doing custom saddle fittings within a three-state area surrounding her Maryland base.

Although Amy travels to a few large hunter shows each year, she specializes in horse trials and events because "I enjoy them the most. The people, in my experience, are really open to new ideas and interested in what's good for their horse. They're happy to be there themselves, and happy to see you there." Amy's own riding was always strictly for pleasure, never competitive, although when she has taken lessons they have been primarily dressage-oriented. She recently gave in to the reality of her business's demands taking precedence in her life and sold her own horse; she just didn't have time to devote to him. Working with horses is what got Amy into this business in the first place, and when she discusses selling her horse, it's clear that it wasn't an easy decision.

"I spent a lot of time preparing myself to do that," she says, "and

I feel okay about it now. I sold him to someone who loves him to death, and who will have a good time with him." It isn't unusual for women to get into a horse-related business because they love riding, only to find that the business becomes so successful that they have little time to ride anymore. But Amy says she definitely plans to have another horse someday, "when I have more help. That's kind of my dream." In working toward that dream, she's begun to make certain changes in the business. For one thing, she plans to cut back on the number of small shows she attends, but will keep her mobile rig and still go to the larger shows. "A mobile business is something that really wears you out," she explains, noting that there is also more competition from larger tack shops than when she first started attending shows. Another venture that she hopes will eventually allow her to spend all or most of her time closer to home is a small mail-order business she is launching. "It'll be a small catalog," she says, "because I really don't want it to get so big I can't keep control of it. I've hired some people for answering the phones, shipping, and receiving, and I'm sure I'll have to hire more, but basically I plan to run the business myself."

Amy's schedule now is somewhat seasonal, beginning with the spring eventing schedule, which runs from March to June, with just a few summer shows. The events are concentrated again from August through October. During the show season the work alternates between taking orders, shipping them out, paying bills, working the shows (she hires help for the bigger shows), and doing saddle fittings in between. During the less busy winter and summer months, she does more traveling for individual fittings, maybe three or four days a week. The larger shows, like the PanAmerican Games or the Rolex/Kentucky Horse Trials, can last a week or more at a time.

To sell saddles requires a thorough knowledge of the requirements of the sports or disciplines you hope to reach, and an understanding

Detail of an English Saddle

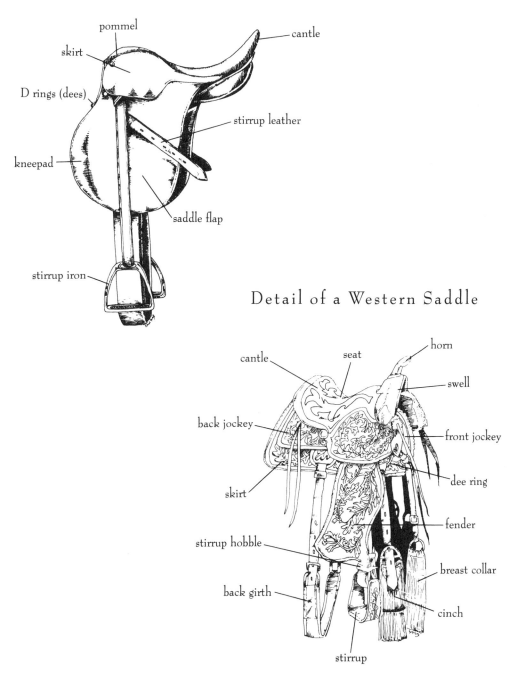

pommel

cantle

skirt

D rings (dees)

stirrup leather

kneepad

saddle flap

stirrup iron

Detail of a Western Saddle

cantle

seat

horn

swell

back jockey

front jockey

dee ring

skirt

fender

stirrup hobble

breast collar

back girth

cinch

stirrup

of the horse's conformation and movement. You need the ability to work with people, business sense, and of course, a knowledge of the saddles themselves. Although Amy sells only English saddles, there is a vast array of English saddles, each designed specifically for a particular sport. A jumping saddle is quite different from a dressage saddle, and an "all-purpose" saddle, often used in combined training, combines some of the features of both. And although all dressage saddles have certain features in common, there are many different models and styles, designed to provide maximum comfort to both horse and rider depending on their individual sizes and body types. There is also a wide price range, reflecting the quality of materials and workmanship that go into the saddle. The best way to learn about English-made saddles, says Amy, is to go to England. Most English saddles are made in the small town of Walsall, and if you go there you can become an apprentice to a master saddler. Since this isn't practical for many people, however, there are alternatives.

"There are saddlers trained in England who are here, and one of them might help you get started," says Amy. She says that one of her suppliers does a lot of saddle fitting, and she learned a lot from him. You can also learn about how saddles are made from books and articles on the subject, and equine massage therapists often know a lot about conformation, movement, and what factors can hinder free movement of the horse. So, although there is no formal training program for learning how to fit saddles properly, the best approach is to find people who can teach you.

"Try to keep an open mind," says Amy, because you may find the information you need in unlikely places. "I would start by looking for a competent saddler and approaching this person for help, information, or possibly an apprenticeship situation."

Once you understand what goes into the making of a saddle, from the tree to the carefully handstitched pigskin seat, you'll have a much clearer understanding of what makes saddles different and which kind of saddle will be most suitable for a particular buyer and her horse. Once you understand the function of classic saddle design, it will be easier to learn how to adapt that basic design to the conformation and activities of any horse-and-rider combination.

Most riders purchase their saddles from a tack shop or mail-order catalog and then try it on their horse to see if it fits. But many excellent horsepeople have only a minimal understanding of how a saddle should fit their horse. That's where Amy's unique mobile unit comes in. For a small fee (about $50, depending on the traveling distance), Amy will come to the barn, check the fit of a rider's existing saddle,

and offer suggestions for a replacement if necessary. She shows the owner how the width of the saddle's tree must be matched to the width and shape of a horse's withers and shoulder, how the center of the saddle should sit level over the horse's center of gravity, and how to place the saddle properly on the horse's back. Amy says that many people put their saddles too far forward on the horse, not understanding that the front edge of the panels on the underside of the saddle should lie just at the edge of the horse's shoulder blades, so as not to interfere with free shoulder movement. And if the tree of the saddle is too narrow or too wide, the saddle will be uncomfortable for both horse and rider. Trying to fix the situation with pads often makes it worse, and in the long run, a horse's health and performance will suffer. Most riders appreciate the peace of mind that comes from knowing a saddle fits both them and their horse correctly before spending anywhere from several hundred to over a thousand dollars to purchase it.

This is a competitive business, but if you can find your own special niche a ready market awaits you. Specializing in a particular discipline or type of horse is one way to find your market, says Amy. Geographic considerations come into play, too, with the western United States offering a less competitive environment than the East at present. In this field, it's not enough to just know horses. The secret to success is to be more businesslike, says Amy, and less a starry-eyed horse lover. Figure out your market first: Who will you sell to? What will your markup be? What will be your costs for doing business? Is it realistic to expect that you can sell enough to eventually make a profit? A business degree certainly wouldn't hurt, she admits, but you can find people who are knowledgeable to advise you. Relatives and friends in business, accountants, and attorneys are all possible sources of information. So is your local Small Business Administration, as well as SCORE—Service Corps of Retired Executives, an organization of business executive volunteers who offer free management counseling to small businesses all over America.

"Be cautious and careful," says Amy. "Figure out how much you must bring in, and set target dates. Even if you don't meet all the targets, at least if things seem to be moving in the right direction you can feel fairly confident to keep going. It can take several years to get a small business off the ground, and you do have to be realistic if you find it just isn't working at all." It's possible to learn as you go, but it's much safer to have a plan. "I didn't do as much advance planning as I would advise others to do, but I wish I had." She adds, though, that she sought out good advisers and was very careful in developing the business. You should plan, she says, to "start tiny and grow gradually. When we started to make a profit, everything went back into the business. Now that profits are increasing, it's all been going into the start-up of the catalog." It may take a few years to begin to make a comfortable income. Amy estimates clearing about $10,000 to $15,000 in the early years, once you reach a point where you don't have to reinvest all your profits into the business. "After my business is no longer growing," she says, "I'd like to think I will eventually make around $30,000 a year."

To succeed at creating your own business, you need patience, determination, and an ability to deal with the present while planning for the future. You need to know about horses, tack, riders, and trainers.

"It takes a certain type of character to succeed at this," says Amy, "and you'll find out pretty quickly if you have it."

11

Bonnie Luther

Farrier

NO ONE IS MORE important to a horseman than his farrier, the horseshoer in whose hands rest a horse's soundness, athletic success, appearance, and comfort. It is unusual, though, for those hands to belong to a woman, so a farrier's career may not occur to women searching for a job with horses. But if you really want to make a difference to horses and their owners, and if you want to learn a skill that will always be in demand as long as horses perform the jobs humans ask of them, consider the farrier's craft. Bonnie Luther knows how much her clients and their horses appreciate her work.

Wild horses have little need for shoes. The delicate structures of their feet are protected by a hard covering of horn, the hoof, which wears naturally at the proper rate and angle as the horse wanders over grassy fields to graze. But since few horses today live this kind of life, protective horseshoes are a necessary invention to ensure the comfort and soundness of horses who jump, race, carry loads over hard and uneven ground, or pull burdens across slippery paved surfaces. Most working horses need to have their hooves trimmed and balanced by a professional farrier about every six weeks. "Farrier" is the correct term for someone who shoes horses, although people often use the term "blacksmith." A blacksmith is a person who works iron into decorative and useful items, but most farriers make only horseshoes. If a horse is shod (wearing shoes), it may need to have the shoes replaced with new ones each time its feet are trimmed. Sometimes the farrier will be able to use the same shoes again if they are not too worn, but in this case the shoes must still be removed, the hooves trimmed, and the shoes reshaped and nailed back onto the horse's hooves. Horseshoes can be made of aluminum or plastic, but most are made of iron, which is heated and shaped to fit the horse's foot and held in place with special nails. The horse's hoof is constantly growing, just as a human's fingernails grow, and like fingernails the hoof can be cut or nailed without causing pain to the horse, as long as the sensitive tissues deep within the foot are not disturbed.

The work of a farrier requires a certain amount of physical strength and agility, and women like Bonnie are proving every day that they have what it takes. For women who love hands-on work with horses, independence, and the outdoors—and for those who are willing to work very hard—it can be the perfect career.

Bonnie has about 300 clients—horses she shoes as needed, about every four to eight weeks, traveling from barn to barn in a specially outfitted pickup, which serves as a portable blacksmith shop. The work keeps her busy from nine to twelve hours a day, six days a week. She is able now to be fairly selective about her clients, but it wasn't always that way. "When you start out," she says, "you have to do anything—wild, crazy horses, working in mud and rain and wind. I wound up shoeing every horse that no one else would do, at first, but then I began to get the opportunity to work for true horsemen who know how to manage horses the right way, and that made a big difference. Horses who are handled properly are a lot easier to work with, and having a safe place to work is nicer too."

Bonnie has always loved horses, and her family owned some by the time she was fourteen. "When I was in high school, we got this book called *The Art of Horseshoeing*, by Gordon Greeley. I read it and decided I'd shoe our horses; why my parents let me try, I'll never know. Anyway, it was a complete fiasco, with me slicing my hand open and probably doing a lot worse to the poor horse. After that we hired someone else to do our shoeing work."

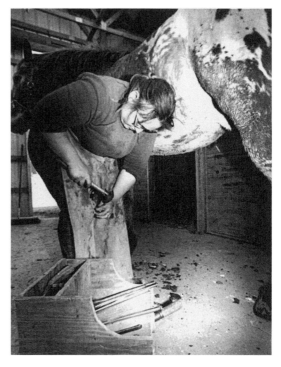

After she graduated from high school, Bonnie traveled and drifted through a series of jobs in factories and offices. By the time she was in her mid-twenties in 1979, she decided she wanted a different direction. Since she'd always wanted to work with horses, she enrolled in an intensive twelve-week course at the Eastern School of Farrier Science in Martinsville, Virginia. "I picked that school because at the time it was one of the few residential schools that even admitted women, and one of the only ones with a women's dormitory," she says. There are approximately twenty horseshoeing schools in the country, all of which are unregulated and operate independently. Courses range from two weeks (sufficient only if you want to "try out" the work or learn to do basic trims on your own horse) to two years (which would prepare you to enter the field as a qualified professional). The Lexington, Kentucky–based American Farriers Association (AFA) offers a current list of schools, as well as a newsletter and listings of local AFA chapters.

A farrier school curriculum combines classroom lectures on theory and basic principles of anatomy and forging with demonstrations and practical training shoeing horses. But Bonnie says the hours of actual practice shoeing were not enough to really prepare students for the work of a farrier. "It doesn't make any sense when you start," she explains, "and there is too much information to absorb all at once. You have to get out in the field and actually start doing it before all the theories and demonstrations begin to make sense." Unfortunately, though, "Nobody wants to use someone just out of school, and you can't blame them, because you really don't know what you're doing at first." So it wasn't so much that being a female farrier was a stumbling block as it was being an *inexperienced* farrier. It was difficult to find horse owners who were willing to take a chance on any farrier fresh out of school. That's the catch, says Bonnie. Being a skilled farrier is something you learn by experience, but it can be very difficult to get the necessary hands-on experience when you first start out. Luckily, Bonnie had some friends who were dealers specializing in inexpensive horses.

"They'd go to the auctions and find horses that were going to be sold for meat. They'd pick out a few that they thought were kind of good looking, put a little time into them, and then try to sell them for a small profit. They gave me my first chance." She took out a loan to buy a truck and basic equipment, following a suggested list from farrier school. Later she found that "a lot of it was a waste of time and money. For example, I started with a coal forge, and then the big thing was gas-powered forges. So I got one of those, but then I found out I didn't like it, so I went back to coal." After spending a lot of money for a fancy new truck, she later went back to buying used trucks, which she "runs into the ground," because she decided she didn't need a flashy vehicle to impress clients: "It's not the truck that shoes the horse; *I* shoe the horse." Bonnie puts about 30,000 miles year on her truck, so while it need not be fancy, it must be reliab'

Traditionally, establishing a farrier business has been a sort of do-it-yourself enterprise. The ancient and mysterious craft was understood by few and supervised by no one, but all that is beginning to change. Through its local chapters, the AFA offers three levels of certification, each involving written (theoretical) and practical tests. Bonnie received her basic certification at the completion of her school training, after passing the required tests. The top level of certification, Journeyman, requires that the farrier have at least two years' experience to be eligible for the exam, and he or she must prove an in-depth command of anatomy and physiology as well as the ability to hand-make shoes, including bar shoes (a special type of corrective shoe that circles the entire bottom of the shoe's foot, including a "bar" that supports the heel). Certification is optional; many people—some of them excellent horseshoers—have never taken the tests and are working as farriers. Most horse owners are unaware that a certification program even exists. This is likely to change, however, as the AFA presses for new standards to raise the overall quality of work within the profession. Required testing and licensing of all farriers may be instituted in the future as a way to ensure that any person trimming and shoeing a horse's feet for pay has the necessary knowledge and training to do a good job.

Bonnie, who has three horses at home, including one shown by her stepdaughter on the 4-H circuit, starts her days early with feeding and barnwork. By seven-thirty or eight she's on the road. "I try to limit it to five horses a day, but sometimes in the summer, when the days are longer, I wind up doing between six and ten. Although I try to be home by five, on those long days sometimes I don't get home until ten at night." She has a shop in her barn at home, and sometimes clients bring their horses to her. Based in a heavily horse-populated area of south-central Pennsylvania, Bonnie shoes all breeds and disciplines: quarter horses, Thoroughbreds, Arabians, hunters, barrel racers, dressage horses, walking horses, trail horses. All of them have different shoeing requirements, which Bonnie has learned by reading books and journals, careful observation, talking to owners, going to various types of events to watch the horses compete, and most important, "noting how a horse is shod when it first comes to me, if I know it came from a professional trainer and was properly shod."

Each horse can take from just a few minutes (for a simple trim of unshod hooves) to several hours (if four new shoes are needed). Some horses wear shoes only on their front feet, since most of the horse's weight is supported by the front feet, while others need them on all four hooves. Sometimes the front shoes will need to be replaced with new ones, while the hind shoes can simply be removed, the hooves trimmed, and the shoes put back on. In other cases the owner may want Bonnie to try a different type of shoe, or the horse may have developed a problem that requires a shoeing change. Most of the shoes are heated in a small forge in the back of the farrier's truck, which creates a concentrated, intense flame. The hot iron can be shaped on the anvil, using various types of hammers and other tools. The farrier will usually make many trips between the anvil and the horse, checking and adjusting the fit of the shoe until she is satisfied, and sometimes the shoe will be "burned" into the horse's foot for a few seconds while it is still hot. This is called "hot shoeing," and some farriers think it gives the shoe a better fit.

Besides the different types of shoes for various riding disciplines, each horse is an individual, with his own particular foot problems and shoeing needs. "I've gotten to the point now where I'm working with some vets on different horses," says Bonnie. Although she has no plans to specialize in corrective shoeing, as some farriers do, still she says, "I'm beginning to understand a lot of the different problems you see, like founder, navicular disease, ringbone, and so on. I try to do a good job for every horse I see, and if a problem comes up, I like to be able to handle it." For some of these problem horses, she makes special "orthopedic" shoes, in eggbar shapes or with wedges or special pads. Differently shaped shoes can provide support to the horse's foot where it is needed, to help keep it comfortable despite minor problems. Some of these conditions can cripple a horse despite everything the farrier and vet can do, but in other cases a good shoeing job can make the difference between a sound horse and one in constant pain.

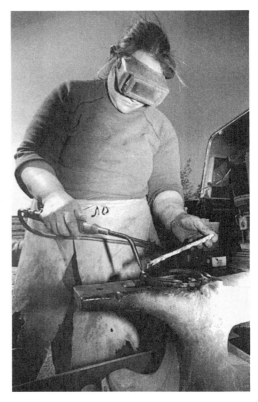

"When I first came out of farrier school, I had all these high ideals," says Bonnie. "I was going to make handmade shoes for every horse I shod. But pretty soon you find out that's not practical, or even necessary." Hand-shaping a ready-made shoe to fit the foot of a horse with no special foot problems is standard practice in the farrier business, but a good farrier can make a shoe from a length of steel bar if the need arises. Sometimes a horse will need a lighter shoe made of aluminum or plastic, or a hoof defect or injury will require special repair techniques using acrylics or other materials. To keep up with new developments in the field, Bonnie, like many of her colleagues, attends clinics and seminars regularly. The AFA sponsors educational programs all over the country throughout the year. But you need to build a certain base of knowledge and experience through practice, says Bonnie, before you can really understand the new ideas presented at seminars.

Income potential for a farrier varies with skill level, location, and horse population. The AFA estimates an average income for a full-time farrier at around $30,000 a year. But since good farriers are in short supply, the only potential limits to your income are skill and commitment, the patience to establish a reputation, and the willingness to work long hours.

Cost of training also varies greatly. A nine-week course at the Eastern School of Farrier Science, for example, costs $2,000 plus board. The majority of the students are males, with an average age of thirty, but usually a quarter to a third of the students are women, and ages have ranged from fourteen to seventy-eight years, according to Eastern's owner and administrator, Danny Ward.

"I'd like to see them apprentice after they leave here," Ward says. "You don't make a master farrier in nine weeks."

Bonnie agrees. "The best thing to do, if you want to become a farrier, is to go to a good school. Then, when you get out, try to find the best farrier you can to work with." She admits that finding an apprenticeship can be difficult, partly because the experienced farrier knows that the work of his apprentice will reflect directly on his own practice. But she insists it's the very best way to start in the business.

"This is a great life for the right person," she says. That person will, above all, love horses and enjoy working with them, even the ones who are difficult. She will be independent, self-motivated, and will enjoy dealing with people as well as horses. "The people have to like you, and they have to be able to communicate with you," she says. She will also be physically strong, because shoeing horses is hard on the legs, knees, and back. She'll enjoy being her own boss, and take pride in her work and satisfaction in the knowledge that she is helping horses to stay sound and healthy.

12

Wendy Vaala

Equine Perinatologist

THE FIVE-WEEK-OLD FOAL is tiny but perfectly formed, from his white-striped nose to his whisk-broom tail, which at this moment is flicking in irritation at the people who are preventing him from latching on to his mother's milk-filled teat. Born prematurely, the sole survivor of a rare twin birth, the well-bred colt has not yet gained enough strength and control to nurse normally without aspirating milk into his lungs, which could lead to life-threatening pneumonia. Despite that, the bright chestnut baby is looking pretty feisty, and the whole staff involved in his care at the University of Pennsylvania's New Bolton Center neonatal intensive care unit is relieved that it looks like he's going to make it. They've all fallen in love with the little quarter horse. When he arrived in the middle of a cold January night, bundled in blankets in the back of his worried owners' station wagon, he was barely breathing, and he's had a lot of ups and downs since then.

Suddenly the foal wheels around, kicks up his silver-dollar-sized feet in a tiny buck, and dashes under his mother's belly, hoping to outsmart his human caretakers. The young woman in jeans, sweater, and sneakers with a stethoscope draped around her neck chuckles delightedly along with the visiting observers. But all the while her mind is ticking off the tests she needs to schedule on this little guy for today. He's the star of the show this morning, but there are three other very sick foals in the unit who need round-the-clock care. Wendy has to check on all of them, plus get the unit ready for another incoming admission due to arrive shortly.

Most young people who love horses consider entering the field of veterinary medicine, but many are discouraged by the prospect of long, expensive years of schooling or the demands of a full-time, traveling practice. What they may not know is that there are many different kinds of opportunities open to veterinarians today, ranging from private practices for small or large animals, wildlife, exotic species, and marine animals to positions in academia, industry, and government. Many practitioners work only with horses, and equine vets may further specialize in a field like internal medicine or surgery, usually in a major teaching and research facility such as the New Bolton Center, part of the University of Pennsylvania School of Veterinary Medicine. It is here that Wendy Vaala, V.M.D., spends much of her time caring for very sick foals in a state-of-the-art intensive care unit. Wendy is an equine veterinarian certified in internal medicine and specializing in perinatology, the branch of medicine dealing with the care of newborns both shortly before and after birth.

For Wendy there *were* long, difficult years of preparation; her hours today are no shorter and her responsibilities even more demanding, but she says that, for her, this is a "fabulous career."

"I was that little girl who always dreamed of owning a horse," says Wendy, who grew up in a small suburban community in Delaware. "I've been fascinated by horses ever since I can remember. My first

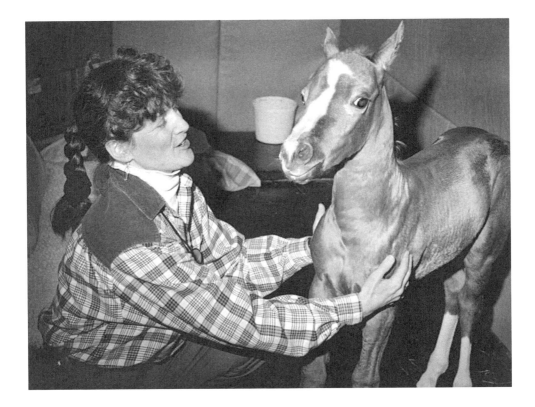

memories are of feeding sugar cubes and carrots to the horses at Tyler
Place, a family resort on Lake Champlain, in Vermont." Back home
in Delaware Wendy's father, who had grown up on a farm in Minnesota, began taking her for pony rides on summer Sundays when
she was about five. Then, she says, she began reading everything she
could find about horses: all the Black Stallion books by Walter Farley,
and all the stories by Marguerite Henry about the wild ponies of
Assateague and Chincoteague islands.

She began riding lessons at age six — "I lived for that weekly lesson." No one else in Wendy's family rode, but she says that "for as
long as I can remember I wished for a 'baby horse' for Christmas.
For many years it never came, but I never stopped asking and hoping." Although not involved with horses, her family was fond of animals in general, and sometimes took in orphaned rabbits and birds.

There was always at least one family dog and cat, and "all my bedtime stories were about animals. I remember all the Thornton Burgess books about animals. So I grew up with a deep respect for all animals, both wild and domesticated."

She also learned to respect the life-saving work of veterinarians, whose skills were often called upon to preserve the health of her very favorite animal. Due to the valuable position of the horse in the mostly rural early American society, equine practitioners were the first professional veterinarians commonly practicing. Until the early part of the twentieth century, when horsepower began to give way to machines, veterinarians spent most of their time caring for the horses on whom the harvest depended. Later, as the horse population dwindled, veterinarians turned to dogs, cats, cows, swine, and other animals to support their practices. But with the revival of horse activities after World War II, equine medicine has steadily grown.

Wendy chose a career in veterinary medicine early, and in the fifth grade visited the New Bolton Center for the first time, to gather information for a school report on veterinary medicine.

"In school, I loved science, biology in particular, and veterinary medicine seemed to be a natural extension of those interests. As a senior in high school I spent six weeks as a volunteer at New Bolton Center. Every lameness exam I saw, every surgery I watched, and every veterinary student I talked to convinced me that this was the only career for me." Meanwhile, Wendy had begun competing in local horse shows, riding on a drill team, and entering local endurance rides, after finally getting her first horse when she was about thirteen.

"But my favorite pastime," she remembers, "was riding across country along the Brandywine River: just me, my horse Scubbin's Star, and my Irish setter." Star went with her to the University of New Hampshire, where the cross-country rides continued, and he remained with her until his death at age twenty-three.

Wendy graduated from the New Bolton Center School of Veterinary Medicine, and has been a veterinarian for fourteen years. Her first year after graduation was spent in private practice, treating small animals as well as large. Then she returned to New Bolton to complete a one-year internship in large-animal medicine and surgery, followed by a two-year residency in large-animal medicine. It was not until the completion of these years of training that she was eligible to become board-certified in internal medicine. She has been on staff at the New Bolton Center since 1981, and she was instrumental in the development of its modern neonatal intensive care unit for sick foals, calves, and other large animals. The new unit opened in 1990, replacing an older facility, and during foaling season can accommodate up to seven foals and three mares at a time. Other large animals like cows, pigs, and even exotic animals like llamas have occasionally been admitted, but most of the patients are horses. A six-stall intensive care unit is connected to the neonatal section.

Wendy's time is divided among seeing and treating patients; teaching veterinary students, residents, and visiting veterinarians; and clinical research. She also lectures to veterinary associations and horse-owner organizations all over the United States and abroad. It's a hectic schedule that requires a lot of energy.

"During foaling season my average day is usually twelve to sixteen hours long. I begin the day by examining all the cases currently in the foal intensive care unit. Then there are various teaching rounds in the morning, and after that the schedule varies according to the cases in the unit. Various diagnostic tests need to be performed, like radiographs [X rays], sonograms [internal pictures made with sound waves using ultrasound equipment], blood cultures [analyzing the blood for microorganisms like bacteria], etc., and throughout the day I remain in contact with both the owners and referring veterinarians associated with each case. So I usually answer what seems to be an endless num-

ber of phone calls. On certain days I give formal lectures to the veterinary students, and during what I jokingly refer to as my 'free' time I try to complete articles I am writing, and also review a book chapter I am editing. I am on call twenty-four hours a day for sick foals, so my schedule and all its careful organization can go out the window as soon as a new emergency arrives." During the three busiest months another veterinarian shares responsibilities for the foal unit, but even so there is rarely a spare moment in Wendy's day.

Veterinary medicine is a relatively difficult field to enter. Since there are only twenty-six veterinary schools in the United States, on average only one out of five applicants is accepted into one of the schools. Often preference is given to residents of the state whose higher education system supports the veterinary school in that state. You must have good grades in college science courses; every veterinary school has a list of particular courses that must be completed during the undergraduate years. Because entrance into vet school is so competitive, you also need to gain practical experience, perhaps working in a related field to demonstrate your interest, dedication, and thorough understanding of your chosen career. Like professional schools of law and medicine, veterinary school is expensive, but if you qualify and are accepted, you will find that financial aid is available.

You'll earn a good living as a veterinarian, although incomes are generally below those of medical doctors. Vets in private, mostly small-animal practices tend to earn the most, but equine practitioners whose patients include valuable racing and breeding stock also do quite well financially, with incomes ranging as high as $100,000 or more. Other well-paid positions exist in industry for those veterinarians with additional advanced degrees in related fields such as nutrition, biomedical engineering, or pharmacology. Feed companies, drug companies, equipment manufacturers, and other horse-related industries all need the expertise of professional veterinarians, as do colleges and universities with agricultural and animal science programs and governmental agencies dealing with animals. The average equine veterinarian, while she will certainly earn a comfortable income, doesn't expect to become wealthy, says Wendy. Both in an academic setting such as Wendy's at the New Bolton Center and in private practice, she estimates income ranges from about $25,000 yearly for someone just starting out up to about $75,000 once a practice is well established.

The equine veterinarian in private practice may log as many miles in a year as a traveling salesman, but the advantages are independence, plenty of challenge and variety every day, and the true satisfaction of helping to keep horses healthy. Educating owners to give their horses the very best care possible is another high point of the job for many vets. For those with a more academic bent, a hospital-based practice like Wendy's involving teaching and research as well as patient care may offer many of the same rewards plus the excitement of being on the cutting edge of new understanding and techniques. Wendy finds great satisfaction in searching for new, better ways to treat everyday horse ailments and injuries. Sometimes the research will involve puzzling new diseases, or rare symptoms that are difficult to diagnose.

One of the best ways to learn more about what it's like to be an equine practitioner is to talk to one; better yet, visit a local equine practice and, if the veterinarian seems agreeable, volunteer your services to help out. Just as being a hospital volunteer can be a way to observe firsthand what a doctor, nurse, or lab technician does, volunterring to help in an equine practice can give you a feel for the reality of being a horse vet. You can locate an equine practitioner in your area through your local phone directory or by writing to the American Association of Equine Practitioners and requesting the current AAEP directory. Most equine veterinarians love their work and will be happy to discuss it with you if you first make an appointment. Work with a veterinarian, whether paid or not, will also help to convince veterinary schools of your sincerity and dedication when the time comes to apply for admission.

It's not for everyone, but "if you enjoy working with animals and people," says Wendy, "then this is a fantastic career."

13

Anne Barclay
Therapeutic Riding Worker

PEOPLE WHO FIND their life's work with horses are rarely motivated by a desire to become wealthy. The majority of horse jobs pay modestly at best, but for some people that's not the point. If you don't need a salary to justify the time you spend with horses or if you have always dreamed of a life with equines but also plan a career in another field, some rewarding opportunities for working with horses may await you. In almost any location in America, there is a need for volunteers to work with horses. The pay is the work itself, and the satisfaction of knowing you are truly making a difference, improving the lives of horses and humans. Therapeutic horseback riding can be one of the most effective forms of treatment for children and adults suffering a wide range of physical and mental difficulties. Therapeutic riding programs are starting and expanding all over the United States, and with this growth comes a need for people who love horses and can assist with the programs.

Anne Barclay has been involved in therapeutic riding for twelve years. She currently oversees a program serving about twenty-five disabled adults and children in Westminster, Maryland. She is a lifelong horsewoman who has always kept horses at her own farm, and at various times in her life has foxhunted, been a dressage and event rider, trail ridden, and bred horses. "I still have a few foals," she says. "My profession was social work, working with mentally disturbed people," says Anne. "So therapeutic riding just seemed to be a natural outgrowth of that work for me." Sometimes health professionals such as physical therapists or psychologists whose avocation is horses find a perfect niche working in therapeutic riding programs, and a few of the larger programs may even offer paid directorships to qualified professionals. A degree in physical therapy combined with a solid foundation in riding could qualify you for a paid staff job at one of the larger equine therapy centers, earning a salary of about $35,000 annually. But more often programs are staffed entirely with volunteers: parents and friends of participants who may have plenty of interest but no background with horses, and horsepeople with a strong sense of community spirit who enjoy working with people of all kinds and whose experience with horses is crucial to the success of any therapeutic riding program.

Therapeutic riding is a form of treatment for a wide range of human disabilities, using the movement and warmth of the horse. It is often recommended for patients with cerebral palsy because it can dramatically relax the spasticity (involuntary contractions) of the muscles. Another benefit is that the patient's position on the horse prevents the rider's legs from crossing, which aids in treatment of this condition. Riding also increases upper-body strength, particularly the muscles that support the head and neck. Many other types of patients have benefited from equine therapy, including people with amputated limbs, those who have suffered strokes or brain or spinal cord injuries, the visually and hearing impaired, and mentally retarded or emotionally disturbed children and adults.

Therapeutic riding got its start in England and Germany about fifty years ago, made its way to North America thirty years ago, and has now grown to about 400 accredited programs in the United States and Canada. Those programs serve from 3,000 to 4,000 riders. In 1992 the North American Riding for the Handicapped Association (NARHA) welcomed 528 new individual members and 73 new operating centers, with requests for information up 92 percent over a two-year period.

"People are becoming more aware of nontraditional forms of therapy for people with disabilities, especially in the light of the Americans with Disabilities Act," says NARHA executive director Bill Scebbi. "ADA makes a statement to the world that people with disabilities should not and do not have to resign themselves to staying indoors all their lives. Therapeutic horseback riding, in addition to its technical therapeutic benefits, gives people with disabilities the opportunity to do something challenging."

Anne says her program could not exist without the support of its loyal volunteers, many of whom are members of the Carroll County 4-H organization and their parents. Sometimes it's hard to tell who is having more fun, the riders or the helpers. But there is a lot more going on in therapeutic riding centers than just fun. Handicapped riders often make great gains in both mental and physical abilities that improve their quality of life both in and out of the saddle. Physically, horseback riding helps patients regain their balance and sense of where their bodies are in space, abilities often lost by people with brain or spinal cord injuries. In addition, abdominal and lower-back muscles are strengthened, and because the horse's motion simulates walking, it helps patients regain that sense of motion themselves. Direct contact with the warmth of the horse's body also helps to relax tightened muscles, allowing them to work more normally. Mental abilities, like following a sequence of ideas or instructions and identifying objects by shape or color, are improved by having riders move

their horses to specific letters posted around the ring in standard dressage fashion. Riders may learn to recognize a figure such as a circle on a card, and then to ride a circle, or they may learn to ride to specific points (the red pole, the green pole) within the ring.

"It's all so rewarding," says Anne, whether the volunteers are working with physically or mentally handicapped clients, although she says, "It's more dramatic with the physically handicapped. One of our group is a paraplegic lady, a former riding professional who was paralyzed from the armpits down in an accident. At first it took four people helping her for her to ride, but now she can go alone with just someone walking alongside. She can trail ride, and she's competed in a dressage show. Last summer we had a junior high–age boy who qualified for the National Special Olympics. That was really exciting." All of the riders who stay with the program gain mobility, self-esteem, and confidence, she says, and they also make a lot of friends.

The horses used in the Carroll County 4-H Riding for the Handicapped program are all donated, as is the case in most programs. Most are very old, and they come in all shapes and sizes, from little Shetland ponies to the big, strapping animals needed to carry a large adult. Some are no longer sound enough to do the work they once performed, although basically sound movement (at least at the walk) is necessary for handicapped riders to derive the full benefits of therapy. But it takes a very special horse to be able to carry these special riders, and the horses seem to understand this.

"They have to get used to everything from wheelchairs to crutches to the rider's involuntary spasms and awkward movements," Anne says. "Sometimes, with heavier patients, it's quite a job to get them up onto the horse, and sometimes special lifts are used. The horses have to take all of this in stride, and of course they must be absolutely trustworthy." A really good therapeutic riding horse will soon learn to take care of his special riders, slowing down or stopping when he feels the rider getting off-balance so both horse and rider can regroup.

Volunteers are welcomed in most therapeutic riding programs. "Anyone can volunteer," says Anne, "although of course they shouldn't be afraid of horses." A solid background of working with horses is a big plus, though, and such a person will be put to work catching, grooming, tacking up, and handling the horses, as well as helping the patients, leading horses, and "sidewalking" (one volunteer walks on either side of the less stable riders to make sure they stay in the saddle, in the proper position). Whatever part you play in a therapeutic riding program, you will be sure of one thing: you are making a difference in someone's life.

14

JoAnne Mauger

Horse Protector

YOU'RE WALKING DOWN a quiet country road, enjoying the view, when you see him: a little spotted pony standing in the middle of a weedy field in the hot midday sun. Flies are clustered around his eyes and ears, and he looks as if he'd like to run away from them, looking for refuge from the heat and bugs. But there isn't any shelter in the field, as far as you can tell, and besides, it seems as if something is wrong with this pony. Not only is he pitifully thin, with protruding ribs and a sharp backbone jutting through wasted flesh and a dull, matted coat; he also seems to be rooted to the spot where he stands, shifting his weight as if to move but unable to lift his feet. You walk closer to the edge of the field, which is enclosed with a single electric wire topped with a strand of rusty barbed wire, and you discover why the little gelding isn't moving: his hoofs are more than six inches long, deformed into ridged stumps that curve up like the runners on a sleigh. As you talk to him softly, the pony pricks his ears a little and takes one painful step in your direction, then sighs and drops his head again, his muzzle almost touching the ground. You look around, but there are no people in sight, and a huge dog chained to the front porch of the farmhouse is eyeing you menacingly. You turn slowly back the way you came, but you keep looking back over your shoulder at the pony. For as long as you can still keep him in your sight he stands, unmoving in the dusty field. You wish you could help him, and for a long time you can't get the memory of the starving, neglected animal out of your mind, but who can you call for help? He's not your pony, and it's none of your business.

JoAnne Mauger has seen countless ponies and horses in this condition, and she and a few other concerned horsewomen have rescued hundreds of them in their work as agents of the Large Animal Protection Society of Chester County, Pennsylvania. "When you love something," she says, "and we all love horses . . . you hate to see them get trashed."

JoAnne's life has revolved around horses ever since she started riding at age nine, but since 1985 there has been a new sense of mission in her equine involvement. That's when a small group of Chester County horsewomen came together to form what would become LAPS—the Large Animal Protection Society. LAPS's sole reason for existence is the protection of horses and other large farm animals from neglect and abuse by enforcing the cruelty laws of Pennsylvania. The women came together when Chester County's Society for the Prevention of Cruelty to Animals asked for donations of feed and halters for nine horses it had seized in a cruelty case. They quickly learned the SPCA's facilities were inadequate for large animals and wanted to help.

What JoAnne and her three fellow cruelty agents see, oftentimes, is not pretty. She has a photo album filled with stark evidence of the ignorance and carelessness of many horse owners, pages of pictures of horses with protruding ribs, saddle sores, deformed feet, and dull, sickly coats. There are sights and memories that stay with her, often long after the animal is gone. One of those was a little gelding who came with a reeking, swollen, infected leg. For three days, JoAnne and her fellow LAPS agents worked on the little horse under veterinary guidance, wrapping and poulticing and hosing the fractured leg. Unfortunately, it was too little, too late, and the gelding couldn't be saved. What got to JoAnne was that, despite his intense pain, and despite the squalid conditions he had lived in for his three short years of life, he had a sweet disposition and he tried hard to cooperate with the people who were, most likely, showing him the first kindness he had ever known.

"Every now and then," says JoAnne, "there are a few that get to you, that you can't forget. This horse was like that. He was put down [put to sleep] on Thursday, and I cried all day Friday. To me, this boy was a solid little citizen and he never even had a chance." Fortunately

most of her stories of horse rescues have happier endings, like that of Ruby, a six-year-old mare whose owner became frustrated that she kept escaping her poorly fenced field. The owner put her in a stall and forgot about her, and the mare was starving when LAPS found her. The agents removed the horse and restored her to health with proper feeding and veterinary care, and then found Ruby a new home where her delighted owners give her the best of care. Another success story is Thomas, a twenty-five-year-old horse who was the group's very first rescue. One of the agents adopted Thomas and he has since lived on her farm. Now fat and healthy, he still bears the scars of the cruel treatment he once received.

"This work frustrates some well-intentioned animal lovers who think they can make everybody else treat their pets the way they would," JoAnne says. "There's too many times you have to walk away from something that is not covered by the law and a lot of people cannot do that." Still, LAPS has handled hundreds of cruelty cases since receiving its state charter in 1985. Only a handful of those cases had to be resolved in court, and fewer still have resulted in the animals' having to be humanely destroyed. Most of the animals are successfully treated and placed in carefully monitored adoptive homes.

LAPS agents have found that ignorance is the root of many cases of abuse and neglect. One of their primary jobs is to educate and advise owners, based on their average of over twenty-five years' experience caring for horses, ponies, and other large animals. But in cases in which the owner is uncooperative, the agents are authorized to issue citations, and the animals may be legally seized.

LAPS maintains a shelter facility to house animals who are in need of rehabilitation and care. Most recover in three or four months with proper medical, dental, and hoof care, and the agents take turns tending to these convalescents. After recovery, the horses and ponies are made available for adoption, with the stipulations that LAPS will conduct regular inspections and that the animals may never be sold. The agency oversees any readoption that may become necessary, to ensure the lifetime security of the rescued animals.

There are no paid staff members in LAPS but, says JoAnne, this fact isn't usually publicized. "Somehow people seem to take you more seriously if they think you're getting paid," she says, but all of the agents are trained, badged, and licensed by the court system of Pennsylvania. That all four current agents are women is not particularly surprising, says JoAnne. "Women almost seem to be more adept at this thing than men. I don't know why, I guess most women take a more conciliatory tone, so they're less threatening. That doesn't bother me, as long as we get the job done." She adds that most humane organizations consider themselves lucky to get anyone knowledgeable to do this time-consuming and emotionally charged work.

"We started from scratch out of our own pockets," says JoAnne of LAPS, which is still funded entirely through private contributions. "We were just normal people who saw what was going on around us and said, 'This is not a tolerable situation.'" Most of the agents maintain full- or part-time jobs outside their LAPS responsibilities, so it is truly a labor of love.

Aside from cruelty investigations, all of the members work hard to educate the public. They make themselves available to speak to groups and clubs, anywhere they can reach potential first-time horse owners. They take information about the care and feeding of large animals to schools and fairs, and try to dissuade people who have no experience with large animals from buying them for pets. "Neglect and abuse happens when people buy a couple of acres in the suburbs and buy a couple of cute, fuzzy lawn mowers," JoAnne explains. "People just don't understand animals need basic care." In the next few years this close-knit and dedicated group hopes to expand into larger geographic areas (they already handle calls from a four-county area).

They plan to make their primary mission education, so they can prevent abuse before it happens.

You get the feeling that JoAnne Mauger feels almost driven to do this work, but to her it is a natural outgrowth of her whole life. It's been a life filled with horses since childhood, although she did not own her own horse until she was twenty-three, when she bought a "very bad" horse for $100. "I was devastated when I was young and my father wouldn't let me have a horse, but now I think it was a good thing, because I got experience, working with people who were good and who taught me. A lot of kids want a horse, but lots of times they're not prepared for it." Her experience with horses is broad: she has worked as a barn manager and a hired hand in large barns and small, with steeplechase horses, hunters, and racehorses. At nineteen she was galloping racehorses for a prominent operation, and with her own horses she's foxhunted and done some competitive trail riding. She started a business offering temporary help for horsepeople: barn-sitting, filling in for sick employees, etc., but she found that jobs were too unpredictable to make it worthwhile. Now she runs a small farm in rural Chester County, Pennsylvania, with her own horse and a few boarder horses, goats, a donkey, and other animals. She spends much of her time screening cruelty calls and handling abuse cases, and you get the feeling she's never been happier.

15

What Else Is There
to Do?

THE WOMEN PROFILED in this book have built careers out of their passion for horses. Many are unusual careers, either because hardly anyone else has thought of doing the same thing or because women are so rarely found working in those positions. Every one of these women imagined a career for herself starting with her own life experiences, interests, and talents, often without a blueprint, job description, or role model. You can do the same thing. There are an almost unlimited number of possibilities for working with horses, either directly or indirectly. Most of those jobs are not easy to find, and some have yet to be invented. Many pay modestly, although some are quite lucrative, and the work isn't always nine-to-five, Monday-to-Friday. If you really love horses, none of this may matter much, compared to the prospect of earning a living working with your favorite animal.

To begin to get ideas for your equine career, first consider all the things a horse needs to stay healthy and happy in the course of a typical year, from feed and shelter to grooming supplies, medicines and fly sprays, shoes, and blankets. Think of all the things an owner uses in caring for the horse, riding, and maybe competing: tack and riding clothes, magazines and books, sport and breed association memberships, veterinary services, horse trailers, trainers, and grooms. The demand for some products and services may wax and wane with changes in the economy, but all horsepeople have basic needs in lean times as well as fat.

WOMEN WHO LOVE horses can be found in all of these fields and more: horse dentists, veterinary technicians, farm managers, grooms, feed specialists, drug researchers, riding-apparel makers, equine writers and public relations specialists, horse show managers, judges, and stewards, riding instructors and trainers, owners of horse transportation businesses, sport and breed association administrators, barn designers and riding arena consultants, horse trailer manufacturers, equine computer program specialists and designers of computer programs, managers of equine retirement homes, equine extension agents, and horse pedigree researchers. One woman handcrafts custom boot bags and saddle covers that she sells through tack shops and at horse shows; another is an attorney who specializes in equine law issues like leasing and liability protection; some are equine insurance representatives; and others sell supplies the horse and horse owner need. Women have created careers as consultants in the field of equine employment, and as producers of equine sales and educational videos. Almost any career has the potential for equine specialization if you think it through carefully and systematically, *and* if you have a horseperson's expertise.

One of the best ways to gain experience with horses, even if you don't have your own, is to volunteer to work for local horse farms, stables, veterinarians, and trainers. Ask questions. The horse world, in some ways, is like a small club, and most professionals are happy to discuss their work if you show that you are interested and serious. The more you know about horses and the people who care for them, the more ideas you will think of for making a career. Never be afraid to hope. What seems like an impossible dream may be the beginnings of a career just waiting to be brought to life.

For More Information

The American Horse Council, 1700 K Street, Suite 300, Washington, DC 20006, (202) 296-4031, is the national trade association for the horse industry. It publishes a newsletter, tax bulletins, horse industry directory, horseman's tax manual, information on scholarships, and a pamphlet listing organizations involved in equine-related education, plus hundreds of horse industry careers, grouped into five categories.

GENERAL INFORMATION ON EQUINE CAREERS AND TRAINING
(You should be able to find these publications in your local library.)

Careers for Horse Lovers. Ronald Trahan. Boston: Houghton Mifflin, 1981.

The Equine Educational Programs Directory. Susan J. Stuska. Bristol, TN: Susan Stuska, 1991.

A Guide to College Equestrian Programs. John F. Manning. Shelburne Falls, MA: Manning Associates, 1985.

The Equine School and College Directory. Ed. Charlotte Maurer. Carmel, IN: Harness Horse Youth Foundation, 1990.

GENERAL INFORMATION ON STARTING A BUSINESS

Small Business Administration, 450 Golden Gate, San Francisco, CA 94102. (415) 556-0860.

Service Corps of Retired Executives, 1441 L Street NW, Room 100, Washington, DC 20416. (202) 653-6725.

Arnold M. Weiner, Consultant Services, 4 Continental Court, Spring Valley, NY 10977. Consultant for those interested in opening a tack shop or similar business.

VETERINARY AND EQUINE HEALTH CAREERS

American Farriers Association, Kentucky Horse Park, 4089 Ironworks Pike, Lexington, KY 40511. (606) 233-7411. Write or call for complete list of farrier schools.

American Association of Equine Practitioners, P.O. Box 55248, Lexington, KY 40507. (606) 233-0147. Directory of licensed equine practitioners.

American Veterinary Medical Association, 930 N. Meacham Road, Schaunburg, IL 60196. (312) 476-8568. Write for information and addresses of veterinary medical schools.

Baltimore School of Massage, Baltimore Holistic Health Center, 6401 Dogwood Road, Baltimore, MD 21207. (410) 744-1892. Courses in various massage techniques that are useful in treating sports-related injuries of horses.

Equissage, P.O. Box 2167, Southern Pines, NC 28367. (800) 843-0224. Free brochure on training program.

Mount Royal College, Calgary, Alberta, Canada. (403) 240-6867. Three-week instructional program in equine soft-tissue massage therapy.

EQUINE ART AND PHOTOGRAPHY CAREERS

Equine Images: The National Magazine of Equine Art, Equine Images Ltd., P.O. Box 916, Fort Dodge, IA 50501. (800) 247-2000, ext. 218.

American Academy of Equine Art, Box 1315, Middleburg, VA 22117. (703) 687-6701.

The Equine Artists' Marketing Guide & Source Directory, Betsy Klieger-Linamen, P.O. Box 2704, Dept. EQ, Gaithersburg, MD 20886-2704. To order send name and address plus $25.00 per book.

Photographer's Market, Writer's Digest Books, F&W Publications, 1507 Dana Avenue, Cincinnati, OH 45207.

Horses in Focus. Rick Maynard. Middletown, MD: Half Halt Press, 1988.

POLICE AND HUMANE LAW ENFORCEMENT CAREERS

American Humane Association, 9725 E. Hampden Avenue, Denver, CO 80231. (303) 695-0811.

Animal Protection Institute of America, P.O. Box 22505, Sacramento, CA 95822. (916) 422-1921.

American Society for the Prevention of Cruelty to Animals, 441 E. 92nd Street, New York, NY 10028.

Hooved Animal Humane Society National Headquarters, P.O. Box 400, Woodstock, IL 60098. (815) 337-5563.

Humane Society of the United States, 2100 L Street NW, Washington, DC 20037. (202) 452-1100.

Large Animal Protection Society of Pennsylvania. (215) 869-9880.

Police Magazine, Hare Publications, 6300 Yarrow Drive, Carlsbad, CA 92009-1597. (619) 438-2511.

Police Times, American Federation of Police, 3801 Biscayne Boulevard, Miami, FL 33137. (305) 573-0070.

THERAPY CAREERS FOR HORSES, RIDERS, AND THE HANDICAPPED

The Alexander Foundation, Philadelphia, PA. (215) 844-0670.

American Center for the Alexander Technique, New York, NY. (212) 799-0468.

Body Synergy Institute, 215 Cherry Lane, Wynnewood, PA 19096.

Centered Riding. Sally Swift. North Pomfret, VT: David & Charles, Inc.

International Movement Therapy Association, P.O. Box 3702, Stanford, CA 94309.

North American Riding for the Handicapped Association, P.O. Box 33150, Denver, CO

80233. (800) 369-RIDE. Write or call for more information and for a list of therapeutic riding centers in your area.

National Foundation for Happy Horsemanship for the Handicapped, Box 462, Malvern, PA 19355. (215) 644-7414.

EQUINE SPORT ASSOCIATIONS

American Driving Society, P.O. Box 160, Metamora, MI 48455. (313) 664-8666.

American Endurance Ride Conference, 701 High Street, Auburn, CA 95603. (916) 823-2260.

American Horse Shows Association, 220 E. 42nd Street, New York, NY 10017. (212) 972-2472.

American Riding Instructor Certification Program, Charlotte Kneeland, P.O. Box 282, Alton Bay, NH 03810. (603) 875-4000.

Carriage Association of America, R.D. 1, Box 115, Salem, NJ 08079. (609) 953-1516. Publishes the *Carriage Journal*.

National Association of State Racing Commissioners, P.O. Box 4216, Lexington, KY 40504. (606) 254-4060. Write or call for complete list of racetracks in the United States.

National 4-H Council, 7100 Connecticut Avenue, Chevy Chase, MD. (301) 961-2934.

Polo Training Foundation, Daniel Scheraga, Field Director. (315) 696-8036. Supports interscholastic and intercollegiate polo programs, funds clinics, maintains film library.

Polo magazine, 656 Quince Orchard Road, Gaithersburg, MD 20878. (301) 977-3900.

United States Combined Training Association, 292 Bridge Street, S. Hamilton, MA 01982. (508) 468-7133.

United States Dressage Federation, Inc., P.O. Box 80668, Lincoln, NE 68501. (402) 474-7632.

United States Equestrian Team, Gladstone, NJ 07934. (201) 234-1251.

United States Polo Association, 4059 Iron Works Pike, Lexington, KY 40511. (606) 255-0593.

United States Pony Clubs, 893 S. Matlack Street, Suite 110, West Chester, PA 19380. (215) 436-0300.

BREED ASSOCIATIONS

American Hanoverian Society, 831 Bay Street, Box 2, Capitola, CA 95010. (408) 476-4461.

American Morgan Horse Association, P.O. Box 960, Shelburne, VT 05482. (802) 985-4944.

American Paint Horse Association, Box 18519, Fort Worth, TX 76118. (817) 439-3400.

American Quarter Horse Association, 2701 I-40 East, Amarillo, TX 79168. (806) 376-4811.

American Trakehner Association, 1520 W. Church Street, Newark, OH 43055. (614) 344-1111.

Appaloosa Horse Club, Box 840, Moscow, ID 83843. (208) 882-5578.

Arabian Horse Registry of America, 12,000 Zuni Street, Westminster, CO 80234. (303) 450-4748.

The Jockey Club (Thoroughbreds), 821 Corporate Drive, Lexington, KY 40503. (606) 224-2700.

ALL-BREED MAGAZINES

The Chronicle of the Horse, Box 46, Middleburg, VA 22117. (703) 687-6341.

Equus, 656 Quince Orchard Road, Gaithersburg, MD 20878. (410) 977-3900.

Horse and Rider, 941 Calle Negocio, San Clemente, CA 92672. (714) 361-1955.

Horse Illustrated, P.O. Box 6050, Mission Viejo, CA 92690. (714) 855-8822.

Horseplay, 11 Park Avenue, Box 130, Gaithersburg, MD 20877. (410) 840-1866.

Performance Horseman (western) and *Practical Horseman* (English), Gumtree Corner, Unionville, PA 19375. (215) 857-1101.

EQUINE SPECIALTY BOOK AND VIDEO PUBLISHERS
(Write or call for a free catalog of books on horse-related topics.)

Equine Research, Inc., Dept. 1, P.O. Box 535547, Grand Prairie, TX 75011. (214) 660-3897.

Half Halt Press, 6416 Burkittsville Road, Middletown, MD 21769. (301) 371-9110.

Pegasus Press, 535 Cordova, #163, Santa Fe, NM 87501. (800) 537-8558.

The Practice Ring, 7510 Allisonville Road, Indianapolis, IN 46250. (800) 553-5319.

Knight Equestrian Books, Boothbay Road, P.O. Box 78E, Edgecomb, ME 04556. (207) 882-5494.

The Horseman's Source, Inc., 8690 Wranglers Way, Colorado Springs, CO 80908. (800) 325-1894. Equestrian videotape sales and rentals.

Glossary of Horse Terms

acupuncture. Method of healing developed nearly 4,000 years ago in China, based on stimulating the body's energy channels with needles, lasers, or chemical injections.

Andalusian. Breed of riding horse originating in Spain. Usual color gray or black, average height 15.3 hands. Intelligent and sensitive, lively, springy movement. Distinctive feature: flat, almost convex head.

Arabian, Arab. Oldest pure breed of riding horse, thought to have originated in Yemen, has had great influence on all other breeds. Most are bay, chestnut, or gray, average height 15 hands, light, graceful movement and speed, and great stamina. Excels as endurance mount. Distinctive feature: concave head with delicate, fine features, flat croup level with back.

barrel racer. Horse used in the western sport or competition of barrel racing, in which horse-and-rider teams race around a course marked with large barrels, requiring great speed and agility.

bay. A horse of medium-brown color with a black mane and tail. There are light bays and dark bays.

bit. Metal mouthpiece attached to a bridle, which allows the rider to control and guide the horse.

break. The process of training a horse in basic obedience and acceptance of saddle and bridle, weight of the rider, and simple commands.

breed. Any horse with a distinct bloodline that can be traced through a registry, such as Arab, Thoroughbred, or Morgan.

breeze. Way of exercising a racehorse, by asking for a brief sprint of less than maximum speed.

bridle. A head harness used to control a horse.

carriage. A four-wheeled, horse-drawn passenger vehicle, often of elegant design.

chestnut. A color similar to bronze or copper, often referred to in the west as "sorrel." *Liver chestnuts* are dirty bronze or pewter in shade. Chestnuts are also little knoblike calluses on the inside of a horse's front legs just above the knee.

Chincoteague pony. A type of small, inbred North American pony that runs wild on certain islands off the Virginia coast.

chiropractic. In the treatment of horses, adjustment of the horse's vertebrae (backbones) to ease back and neck soreness, stiffness, and unusual lamenesses.

class. At a horse show, riders and horses compete in "classes" based on the age of rider or horse, height of jumps, or whether judging is based on performance of horse or rider, such as Adult Amateur Hunter, Children's Hunter, Junior Equitation over Fences, etc. A horse-and-rider team may enter several classes in a day's competition.

colic. Common digestive disorder of horses, with symptoms ranging from mild to fatal.

There are many causes, including poor feeding practices, excessive fatigue, intestinal obstruction, parasites, or stress.

conformation. A horse's build or physique — the sum total of his parts and their relationship to each other.

crest. The top of a horse's neck.

croup. The rump of a horse.

discipline. A branch of knowledge or teaching. In riding, a particular sport or type of riding, like dressage or eventing.

draft horse. Horse originally bred for farm work, especially plowing. Characterized by a powerful build.

dressage. Considered the most refined form of flat riding (not involving jumps), in which a horse is trained to move in perfect balance with lightness and ease. A systematic training method; the highest levels usually require years of training to master.

endurance riding. A riding discipline in which horse-and-rider teams travel over a specific route, often more than fifty miles, within a specific time limit. Judging is based on the horse's physical condition at the end of the ride as well as speed. Arabs are generally the most successful breed, although others do well.

equestrian. Relating to horseback riding or riders. One who rides horses or performs on horseback.

equine. Of, relating to, or characteristic of a horse.

equitation. The art of riding.

eventing. Also known as *three-day eventing* or *combined training*. A riding discipline in which horse and rider compete in at least three phases: dressage, endurance (which involves cross-country riding over obstacles), and stadium jumping.

farrier. One who shoes horses.

filly. A female horse under the age of four.

fittings. Parts of an English saddle that can be separated from the saddle, such as stirrup leathers, stirrups, and girth. See diagram, p. 59.

foal. A newborn horse of either sex.

forge. To form metal, as in horseshoes, by heating and beating or hammering into shape. Also, in horses, a faulty way of moving in which the rear hoof strikes the toe of a front hoof, most likely to occur at a trot, causing a clicking noise. This is caused by poor balance or overextending.

founder. Also known as *laminitis*. An inflammation of a sensitive tissue in the hoof. In acute cases the sole drops down and separates from the hoof wall. It is caused by overheating, overfeeding, and overworking; it can become a chronic condition, causing lameness.

gelding. A castrated, or gelded, male horse. Gelding is the removal of the testicles, which results in lower male hormone levels, allowing stallions to be safer, more manageable riding horses.

groom. To clean and brush a horse. Or, a person employed to take care of horses.

halter. A rope or leather headpiece with a noseband, cheek strap, and occasionally a headband, used for tying or leading a horse.

hand. A standard of equine measurement. Four inches equals one hand. Therefore, a 17-hand horse would be five feet, eight inches, measured from the bottom of the front hoof to the top of the withers.

harness. The gear or tackle with which a draft animal pulls a vehicle or an implement.

harrow. To break up and level with an implement called a harrow, usually pulled behind a tractor. Most riding rings require regular harrowing.

homeopathy. Alternative medical treatment that involves giving tiny amounts of a substance that in larger doses would cause the very symptoms being treated, in order to help the body's natural defenses fight the disease or injury.

hoof. The horny sheath covering the toes or lower part of the foot of mammals like horses, oxen, or deer. Commonly used to refer to the foot of a horse.

horse trials. Competitions in the discipline of combined training or eventing.

hot walker. A person employed to walk overheated racehorses after training or racing sessions, until the horse's body temperature returns to normal. "Walking hots" is what a hot walker does.

hunter. A horse of any breed used for fox-hunting, most often a Thoroughbred or Thoroughbred cross. Also refers to a *show hunter,* a horse that competes in horse shows that require the horse to jump a course of fences similar to obstacles that would likely be found by a foxhunter, but usually set up in a ring.

jockey. The person who rides a racehorse in races.

jumper. Any horse who has been trained to jump, either in the ring, on the hunting field, or over a steeplechase course. A *show jumper* competes over courses of fences, usually set up in a ring, at horse shows. Jumper fences are similar to hunter fences, but they are considerably higher and wider, and the horse must jump the course as fast as possible, without knocking down any of the fences.

lameness. Any condition which causes pain or difficulty in movement.

mare. A mature female horse (over the age of four).

Morgan. A breed of horse originated in New England in the eighteenth century, descended from one particular stallion known as the Justin Morgan Horse. Morgans can be any color, average about 15 hands in height, and have a short, active stride and great stamina. Very versatile, used for riding and harness work.

navicular disease. Disintegration of the navicular bone of the horse's foot, may be caused by conformation defects or over-work on hard surfaces.

neonatology. Branch of medicine involving newborns. In equine veterinary medicine, the art and science of treating the medical problems of foals.

open shows. Horse shows open to anyone, not restricted to a particular discipline, breed, or membership in an organization.

paddock. A fenced area, usually near a stable and fairly small, used for grazing and exercising horses.

Paint. Not a true breed, but a recognized color breed, with white splashes on black or brown, developed by Native Americans as a riding horse.

Percheron. French draft horse breed, one of the most popular work horses in the world. Gray or black, average height 16.1 hands or more. Well-proportioned, with relatively small, fine head and finer-boxed legs than those of other draft breeds. Popular for carriage work.

perinatology. The treatment and study of conditions relating to the birth process.

poll. The uppermost point of a horse's neck behind the ears.

pony. Any horse under 14.2 hands. Divided

according to height into small, medium, and large ponies.

Pony Club. International organization begun in England in 1929 to prepare young children for the sport of hunting on horseback. United States Pony Clubs were organized in 1953. Members are taught all phases of riding, as well as horse care and stable management.

purse. Prize money in a competition such as a horse race.

quarter horse. Breed developed in America as a quarter-mile sprinter and ranch horse, descended from the Thoroughbred stallion Janus, currently has the largest number of registered horses of any breed in the world. Any color, average height 15 hands, stocky build with powerful hindquarters, surefooted with great acceleration. Versatile, used in racing, rodeo and ranch work, polo, and all types of English riding.

reins. Long, narrow leather straps attached to each end of the bit of a bridle and used by a rider or driver to control a horse.

ringbone. A bony enlargement on a horse's pastern (ankle) bones, often resulting from overwork. Often causes chronic lameness.

saddle. A leather seat for a rider, secured by a girth. See diagram, page 59.

schooling. Training of a horse. Begins at birth when a horse is taught to lead, and later to stand tied and respond to voice commands and riding aids (cues) for the various riding disciplines.

shod. A horse that has had metal shoes attached to his feet with special nails.

show. To show a horse is to enter and/or ride him in an equestrian competition, such as a hunter-jumper show, a dressage show, or a breed show.

show horse. A horse specially bred, trained, and groomed to compete in a horse show.

sound. In a horse, free of any abnormality in structure or function that would interfere with usefulness.

stallion. A mature male horse used for breeding.

tack. Bridle, saddle, and other equipment used in riding and handling a horse.

Thoroughbred. Breed of horse developed in England in the seventeenth century from Arabian ancestry, now the most valuable breed in the world. May be any solid color, average height 15.3 hands. Fast and athletic, excels in racing and all English riding disciplines.

trail horse. A horse used exclusively for pleasure riding or trail riding, not show. Often called a hack or pleasure horse. Horses that compete in the sport of *competitive trail riding* require special training and conditioning.

walking horse. Common expression meaning Tennessee Walking Horse, a breed developed from a variety of U.S. breeds for the purpose of carrying plantation owners in the nineteenth century. Any color, average height 15.2 hands, comfortable paces and high-stepping gaits with a smooth, fast running walk.

warmblood. A type of horse developed from cross-breeding coldblooded (draft horse) breeds with hotblooded (Thoroughbred or Arabian) breeds. There are many different types of warmbloods developed in various European countries over many years.

withers. The bony ridge above the horse's shoulders.

yearling. A horse of either sex that is a year old on January 1 of a given year.

Index